The **Future of Scholarly Communication**

Edited by
Deborah Shorley and **Michael Jubb**

facet publishing

© This compilation: Deborah Shorley and Michael Jubb 2013
   The chapters: the contributors 2013

Published by Facet Publishing,
7 Ridgmount Street, London WC1E 7AE
www.facetpublishing.co.uk

Facet Publishing is wholly owned by CILIP: the Chartered Institute of
Library and Information Professionals.

British Library Cataloguing in Publication Data
A catalogue record for this book is available from the British Library.

ISBN 978-1-85604-817-0

First published 2013

Text printed on FSC accredited material.

Typeset from editors' files in 11/14.5 pt Garamond and Frutiger by
Facet Publishing Production.
Printed and made in Great Britain by CPI Group (UK) Ltd,
Croydon, CR0 4YY.

Contents

Preface

Scholarly communication is in ferment. *The Future of Scholarly Communication* aims to provide an overview of this huge and complex topic, and to identify and evaluate current and future trends.

The process of generating, publishing and disseminating academic research is (maybe needlessly?) complex, so in selecting our contributors we have sought to include players from as broad a spectrum as possible. Of course the different players reflect different interests: some seek to protect the status quo; others are determined to disrupt it. In any case, the stakes are high.

This debate plays out on a global stage, and no country can manage its scholarly communication in isolation. So, while the contributors to this volume are mostly from the UK, we charged them with taking the broad view. We are grateful to them all for their wide-ranging and thoughtful contributions.

Only the foolish would dare to predict exactly what the future holds for scholarly communication. But one thing is certain: it is far too important to leave to chance.

Deborah Shorley and Michael Jubb

Acknowledgement

We are very grateful to Sharona Rowe (Imperial College London), who managed this project from start to finish. Her calm and cheerful efficiency made our task as editors far easier.

We couldn't have done it without her.

Michael Jubb and Deborah Shorley

Contributors

Katie Anders is a consultant at the Postdoc Development Centre at Imperial College, London. She specializes in research examining organizational culture and its impact on workplace experiences. Katie has a Masters in social research from the University of Warwick. She has conducted ESRC-funded research into the experiences of Muslim police officers in English constabularies, and has worked on projects for the Fundamental Rights Agency and the European Commission. Most recently, Katie helped to research and write a series of good practice guides helping early-career researchers to maximize their creativity.

Richard Bennett is currently Vice President for Institutional Sales at Mendeley, and has spent the last 15 years working in the publishing industry. After graduating with a degree in Biomedical Chemistry, he started his publishing career with EMAP, before moving into digital media with BioMedNet. He spent ten years in New York working in various positions: first for Elsevier Science, and then Springer Science + Business Media. At Springer he was responsible for setting up and managing the Americas Licensing group and specialized in the strategic development of the Springer eBook programme, before moving back to Europe as Vice President Sales for NW Europe and Africa. He currently resides in the Netherlands.

Mark L. Brown has been University Librarian at the University of Southampton since 2001. He led the development of the institutional repository strategy at Southampton, has led a range of large-scale digitization projects and is currently developing the institutional service model for research data management. Chair of RLUK between 2007 and

2011, he was responsible for drafting the current RLUK Strategic Plan and is currently leading the strand on 'Redefining the Modern Research Library'. He has also acted as project director for several JISC-funded repository projects, is an advocate of the green Open Access model, and has been a member of several JISC committees and working groups. He is currently the RLUK representative on the EDINA Board.

Ian M. Carter's career has spanned the capital engineering industry, an interdisciplinary research centre and university administration and management. He is a Chartered Engineer and a member of the Institution of Engineering and Technology and of the Chartered Management Institute. Ian is currently the Director of Research and Enterprise at the University of Sussex, where he is responsible for the research and knowledge exchange portfolio, including all aspects of the research lifecycle. He is the Chair of the Association of Research Managers and Administrators (UK) and is a leading member of the Brunswick Group. He is a Distinguished Faculty member of the Society of Research Administrators International. He has served on a number of committees and working groups, for Research Councils UK, the Scottish and English Funding Councils, and Universities UK. Previously, he worked at the University of Liverpool (2005–8), the University of Glasgow (1992–2004), the SERC-funded Engineering Design Research Centre (1990–93) and for NEI Parsons (1983–90).

Ellen Collins is a Research Consultant at the Research Information Network, where she has initiated, developed and managed projects in a range of areas relating to researchers' information behaviours. She is particularly interested in how academic researchers adapt their practices to engage with new technologies and has worked on a number of projects looking at researchers' use of Web 2.0 technologies. She is also interested in the differences between information behaviours in academia and in other research-intensive sectors. She is currently working on OAPEN-UK, a collaborative research project to explore Open Access scholarly monograph publishing in the humanities and social sciences.

Fiona Courage has worked in Special Collections at the University of Sussex Library since 2000 and is responsible for the care and accessibility of its archives, manuscripts, art and rare book collections. These collections include the Mass Observation Archive, the papers of Leonard and Virginia Woolf and the papers of Rudyard Kipling. Her role includes ensuring the provision of research and learning support, and outreach activities relating to the collections. As Curator of the Mass Observation Archive she is responsible for overseeing the continued acquisition of data through the Mass Observation Project and other related projects. Fiona is actively involved in various projects relating to archival collections and educational and research access to such materials. She has presented papers on the Mass Observation Archive at conferences and venues around the UK, USA, Europe and South Korea and was awarded a University of Sussex Teaching Fellowship in 2010 to research innovative teaching activities in several UK and US universities using archival and manuscript collections.

Liz Elvidge is the Head of the Postdoc Development Centre at Imperial College, London. She has a PhD in Glacial Geomorphology and did postdoctoral work in Magnetostratigraphy. Liz has worked at five different UK universities, including Cambridge, where she was Head of Academic Staff Development. She is the editor of two books: *Exploring Academic Development in Higher Education: issues of engagement* (Jill Rogers, 2004) and *Exploring Good Leadership and Management Practice in Higher Education: issues of engagement* (Jill Rogers, 2006). Liz provides support for the 2000 postdocs and research fellows at Imperial and is particularly interested in individual mentoring and coaching schemes for female postdocs.

Jane Harvell is Head of Library Academic Services at the University of Sussex Library, where she is responsible for Learning and Teaching, Research and Special Collections. Before joining the University, she worked in a range of positions and with a number of significant collections at the British Library and the LSE Library. She is an acknowledged expert on devising alternative models for library services and collections when resources are scarce. Jane is particularly interested in the potential for developing non-traditional collaborative relationships between scholarly publishing and academic libraries and archives. She is on the editorial board of *The Serials Librarian*, is a member of the UKSG main committee, on the JISC Journals Archives Advisory Board and on several publishers' Library Advisory Boards.

Michael Jubb is Director of the Research Information Network (RIN). He has held a variety of posts: as an academic historian; an archivist at the Public Record Office; at the Department of Education and Science; Deputy Secretary of the British Academy; and Deputy Chief Executive of the Arts and Humanities Research Board (AHRB) from 1998 to 2005. Since then he has been Director of the RIN, a research and policy unit focusing on the changing needs and behaviours of the key players in the scholarly communications landscape: researchers (in all disciplines), research funders, publishers, libraries and universities. Since 2006 Michael has been responsible for over 30 major reports on key aspects of the scholarly communications landscape, ranging from researchers' use of libraries and their services, through changes to cataloguing and discovery services, to analyses of the economics of scholarly communications, and how they are changing.

Robert Kiley is Head of Digital Services at the Wellcome Library. Currently, Robert is taking a leading role in the implementation of the Wellcome Trust's Open Access policy. He oversees the development of the UK PubMed Central and acts as the Trust's point of contact for *eLife*, the new top-tier, Open Access research journal launched in 2012 with the support of the Howard Hughes Medical Institute, the Max Planck Society and the Wellcome Trust. He has written a number of books including *Medical Information on the Internet: a guide for health professionals* (3rd edn, Churchill Livingstone, 2003), *The Doctor's Guide to the Internet* (RSM, 2001), *The Patient's Internet Handbook* (RSM, 2002) and the *Nurses Internet Handbook* (RSM, 2005).

Mike McGrath read Maths at what is now City University and started work at Brymbo steelworks in 1961 in operational research. He then worked as a bricklayer before joining the Department of Egyptian Antiquities at the British Museum in 1969, where he worked on the 1972 Tutankhamun exhibition and catalogued the Department's collection of 70,000 objects. Transferring to the British Library on its creation in 1974, he worked in many roles, finally retiring in 2001 as Head of UK Marketing. Mike edited *Interlending and Document Supply* and remains active in document supply matters. He has spoken at many conferences over the last 20 years, including the Nordic ILL conference in 2010, the Forum for Interlending (FIL) and the International Federation of Library Associations and a number of the biennial Interlending & Document Supply (ILDS) conferences. He was the marketing officer for FIL until 2008, and for several years ran a document supply workshop at the UKSG (United Kingdom Serials Group) conference.

David C. Prosser became the Executive Director of Research Libraries

UK (RLUK), the representative body for the UK's leading research libraries, in March 2010. Before moving to RLUK, he was, from 2002, the founding Director of SPARC Europe, an alliance of over 110 research-led university libraries from 14 European countries advocating new models of scholarly communication. Previously, he spent ten years in science, technical and medical journal publishing for Oxford University Press and Elsevier Science. During this time he was involved in all aspects of publishing, from production of print and electronic journals through to their editorial and financial management. Before becoming a publisher David received a BSc and PhD in Physics from Leeds University.

Henry S. Rzepa is Professor of Computational Chemistry in the Chemistry Department of Imperial College, London. Dr Rzepa has given many invited and keynote talks around the world about his research, which have made full use of the internet by being both online and promoting interactivity. For the last four years he has also communicated his science in the form of 220+ posts that have appeared on his blog 'Chemistry with a Twist'. Dr Rzepa is the recipient of the Royal Society of Chemistry 1995 Joseph Loschmidt prize for research in the area of Physical Organic Chemistry, the 2002 Pzifer award for teaching excellence in organic chemistry and the American Chemical Society 2012 Skolnik award (jointly with Dr Murray-Rust) for his contributions to chemical informatics.

Roger C. Schonfeld leads the research and consulting efforts at Ithaka S+R, focused on scholarly behaviours and the changing role of the academic library. Previously, Roger was a research associate at the Andrew W. Mellon Foundation. There he collaborated on *The Game of Life: college sports and academic values* with James Shulman and William G. Bowen (Princeton, 2000). He also wrote *JSTOR: a history* (Princeton, 2003), focusing on the development of a sustainable, not-for-profit business model for the digitization and preservation of scholarly texts. Roger received a BA in English Literature from Yale University.

Deborah Shorley was until 2012 Director of Library Services at Imperial College, London. An active member of her profession, Deborah frequently contributes to national and international conferences and in 1998 was awarded the Library Association's Charter Centenary Medal. She has been Head of UKRR (UK Research Reserve) since 2007, and was until recently Chair of MIMAS, a member of JISC Collections Board, on the Board of LIBER (Ligue des Bibliothèques Européennes de Recherche –

Association of European Research Libraries) and a member of the Conseil Scientifique of ABES (Agence Bibliographique de l'Enseignement Supérieur). She was elected to the Research Libraries UK Board in 2008. She currently acts as Scholarly Communications Adviser to Imperial.

Vincent S. Smith is a cybertaxonomist at the Natural History Museum, London, applying computer technologies and the web to the study of taxonomy and biodiversity. Vincent leads the Museum's science informatics activities. These include new approaches to digitizing some of the Museum's 70 million specimens and the development of virtual research environments supporting several hundred taxonomic research communities worldwide. As an entomologist Vincent specializes in the coevolution of parasitic lice and their avian and mammalian hosts. His recent taxonomic studies include work on the evolutionary history of Galapagos mockingbird lice, dating the diversification of lice across mammals and birds, and the origins and evolution of human lice.

John Wood is currently Secretary-General of the Association of Commonwealth Universities and an honorary professor at Imperial College, London. He is a materials scientist by background and has been Dean of Engineering at Nottingham University, and Principal of the Faculty of Engineering, Imperial College. In between these posts he was the chief executive of the Council for the Central Laboratories of the Research Councils, which is responsible for running major science facilities in the UK and elsewhere. He was a founder member of ESFRI, the European Strategy Forum on Research Infrastructure and subsequently became chair, producing the first European roadmap for large-scale infrastructures. In 2007 he was elected chair of the European Research Area Board. He chaired the European Commission's high-level group on the future of scientific data, producing the report *Riding the Wave* in 2010. He is a non-executive director of a number of companies and chair of the Research Information Network. He holds a PhD from Cambridge University and is a Doctor of Metallurgy from Sheffield University. He is a fellow of the Royal Academy of Engineering, a Commander of the British Empire for services to science and was made an Officer of the Order of Merit by the Federal Republic of Germany.

Introduction: Scholarly communications – disruptions in a complex ecology

Michael Jubb

The scholarly communications system has undergone a series of profound changes in the last decade, and change continues apace. Indeed, this book comes at a time when governments, research funders, learned societies and universities, as well as researchers themselves, are showing unprecedented levels of interest in how researchers communicate their findings. In the UK, the Finch Report,[1] the government's response to it[2] and the policies announced by the Research Councils[3] have signalled a sharp acceleration in moves toward Open Access (OA). In Europe, the EU Commission has announced that OA will be a requirement for all publications arising from research funded under the Horizon 2020 programme, and that it will introduce a pilot scheme on access to and reuse of research data.[4] It has also recommended that governments of the member states should introduce policies for OA to both publications and data arising from publicly funded research.[5] In the USA, the White House Office of Science and Technology Policy issued in February 2013 a policy memorandum directing Federal agencies to develop plans to make the published results of federally funded research freely available to the public within one year of publication and requiring researchers to manage the digital data resulting from research.[6]

Such developments indicate how important it is now to find ways to improve the efficiency and effectiveness of communications both between researchers themselves and between the research community and the many other people and organizations who are interested in their findings. Effective communication is essential if we are to reap the full benefits – in the form of tangible contributions to social welfare and economic growth, and also to the intellectual and cultural life of nations – that can and should arise from the substantial investments that governments, charities and others make in research.

The development of effective channels of communication between researchers across the globe has underpinned the growth in our understanding of the world for at least 350 years. The communication of theoretical and empirical findings through scientific journals and other publications has been at the heart of the scientific and broader research enterprise since Henry Oldenburg, the first Secretary of the Royal Society, created its *Philosophical Transactions* in 1665, defining its core functions as:

■ registering research findings, their timing, and the person(s) responsible
■ reviewing and certifying the findings before publication
■ disseminating the new knowledge
■ preserving a record of the findings for the long term.

The ways in which journals fulfil those functions have been transformed over the past 20 years; and their central position in the wider communications system is increasingly being called into question, for at least two reasons. First, as the Royal Society notes in its recent report on *Science as an Open Enterprise*[7] there is a growing gap between the formal publication of research findings in journal articles and the presentation of the data on which those published findings rely. As researchers have gained the ability to generate and analyse unprecedented volumes of data in the course of their research, both journals and authors have faced increasing difficulties in seeking to present that data for scrutiny and reuse within the confines of a journal article. Various initiatives are now in hand to try to address those difficulties, and three of the chapters in this book (Henry Rzepa, Vincent Smith, and John Wood) set out some of the issues and challenges. Second, some researchers are showing increasing interest in the potential of the internet, particularly through the use of social media, for communication directly with each other and with the wider world, thus eliminating altogether the use of intermediaries such as publishers and libraries. As Ellen Collins shows, the use of social media is generally seen as a supplement to, rather than a replacement for, formal publication of findings in journals; and Katie Anders and Liz Elvidge explore some of the reasons why younger researchers may tend to choose traditional means of communicating their research. Nevertheless, social media do mean that journals are part of a more complex environment than was the case even five years ago.

Complexity and the difficulties of foresight are among the recurrent themes of this volume. It covers a wide range of issues of concern to all those with a stake in the scholarly communications process: governments and funders, universities and research institutes, publishers and librarians, researchers and other academics, and the host of people and organizations who are interested in research and its results. We cannot hope to cover all the relevant topics: there is relatively little, for instance, about the challenges that authors, publishers and libraries face in sustaining the role of monographs in the communication of research. But we hope that the matters considered in the chapters that follow will stimulate further discussion and debate.

Varying behaviours, attitudes and interests

This introduction sets the scene by outlining some of the underlying issues and developments that we see shaping the changes in the complex ecology of research and communications in the second decade of the 21st century. That ecology may be characterized as a set of systems, processes and activities involving many different groups of players who interact dynamically with each other and who fulfil complementary but overlapping roles. The ecosystem and the processes that it supports and generates are enriched by the range and diversity of the interactions; and they work most effectively when the activities and roles of the different players are clearly defined and understood. But the digital revolution and the associated changes in activities and behaviours mean that the ecology of scholarly communications – which had seen relatively slow and steady evolution over 200 years – has over the last decade or so experienced rapid and disruptive change.

These changes are but part of a wider context of developments in the digital world: jockeying for position, on a global scale, between content providers, device companies, packagers, aggregators, delivery platforms, bandwidth suppliers and so on, all seeking a competitive edge. Mobile access anywhere and at any time to content of all kinds, tagged with metadata, fully searchable and interwoven with a rich array of other multimedia, is becoming a general expectation; and interactivity and interrelationships with social media are developing fast. There is thus a need to rethink and reconfigure working patterns and practices. But few individuals or organizations can see clearly what the research communications landscape will look like in 10 or 20 years' time.

It is therefore timely to examine how the behaviours and the interests of the different players interact with each other; how the production and consumption of research – with communication at the interface between them – relate to wider political, legal, social and economic developments; how such wider political, social and economic forces affect the choice of policies, especially those relating to distributional conflicts; and how organizations, individuals and groups have sought, and are seeking, to effect change.

For while there is a consensus that the different groups of stakeholders and players in the research communications landscape will continue to encounter disruptive change over the next few years, their motivations and interests in responding to such changes are unlikely to be entirely congruent.

1   *Researchers* are at the heart of the scholarly communications system, and as the chapters by Henry Rzepa, Katie Anders and Liz Elvidge, Vincent Smith, Ellen Collins, and Roger Schonfeld show, their behaviours and attitudes are changing. They need speedy and effective publication and dissemination of research findings. As authors, they are interested in securing publication in high-status journals which maximize their chances of securing high impact and credit for their work, of winning the next research grant and of advancing their careers. As readers and users they are interested in speedy access, free at the point of use; ease of navigation; and the ability to use, and reuse, content with as few restrictions as possible.

2   *Universities* and other research institutions, as Ian Carter shows, need to maximize their research performance and income, and the visibility and impact of their research, but also to bear down on costs and reduce expenditure where they can. Research-intensive universities pay large sums to secure access to the large numbers of scholarly books and journals relevant to their work; but they could face additional costs as a result of a shift to OA publishing funded by author-side payments. Smaller and less research-intensive universities could see reductions in costs as a result of such a shift.

3 *Research funders* need, as Robert Kiley discusses, to secure the maximum impact from high-quality research, and thus to ensure that publications arising from work that they fund are widely accessible – across the global research community as well as all other communities interested in the results – with as few restrictions as possible. Like universities, they need to bear down on costs.

4 *Libraries* – in the HE sector in particular – need to maximize the number of books, journals and other research publications that they can provide for their readers, at the lowest possible cost. Librarians have been in the vanguard in seeking to limit increases in the costs of journals and in promoting the development of repositories. They are also – as Mark Brown shows – developing their roles to provide new services to researchers in an information environment that has changed fundamentally in the last decade.

5 *Publishers* come in many different guises: those that publish thousands of titles and others that publish but one; the commercial and the non-commercial; university presses and learned societies; and OA and subscription based, with many operating both models. Richard Bennett discusses how publishers seek to sustain and develop services for the effective publication and dissemination of research papers and books that are underpinned by peer review. Both subscription-based and OA publishers need to secure the revenues that enable them to offer high-quality services to authors and to readers/users. For subscription-based publishers, developments such as repositories – particularly if embargo periods and other restrictions on use and reuse rights are reduced – are a source of great concern because such initiatives may undermine their business models and prevent them from recouping their costs. For OA publishers, such developments are essentially immaterial because those that rely on article-publishing charges (APCs) recoup their costs up front; repositories simply provide an additional channel for the dissemination of the articles that they publish.

6 *Learned societies* need to sustain their support both for the publication and dissemination of high-quality research in the disciplines they represent, and also for their work in promoting and supporting scholarship and in helping to nurture and sustain strong research communities in those disciplines. Any risks to the surpluses that they

secure through their publications also imperil their wider activities, which their publication surpluses currently fund.

In such an ecology of interlocking but competitive relationships and dependencies, tensions are inevitable; and it is not surprising that the future of scholarly communications has been the subject of fierce debate and conflict. Nor is it likely that all the tensions will be resolved in the near future.

Research and researchers

There are some 6 million researchers in the world, and this figure continues to increase. This growth reflects significant increases in expenditure on research and development (R&D), particularly by governments. Across the 34 members of the Organisation for Economic Co-operation and Development (OECD), for example, gross expenditure on R&D increased by over 60% in real terms in the ten years to 2008, and in major research countries it has tended to exceed the rate of growth in gross domestic product. Up to 2008, therefore, across OECD countries as a group, R&D grew as a proportion of the economy as a whole: from 1.9% in 1981 to 2.3% in 2008.[8]

Of course, only a proportion of R&D expenditure is devoted to the basic and applied research that results in the kinds of findings reported in scholarly books and journals. Governments are the major funders of such research; and they have increased – or at least sought to protect – their budgets for investment in research because they see it as an essential underpinning for a successful modern economy and society. In the USA, for example, the federal budget for basic research increased by 28% in real terms between 2000 and 2009, including the stimulus provided by the American Recovery and Reinvestment Act 2009.[9]

The result has been a sustained increase in the amount of research undertaken, and in its outputs. Much of the focus is on science, medicine and technology, but there have been increases in the social sciences and humanities too; and, as Fiona Courage and Jane Harvell discuss, profound changes in how research is undertaken in such disciplines. The number of articles published in journals across all subjects and disciplines has been growing in recent years at a rate of nearly 4% a year, so that in 2010 over

1.9 million articles were published,[10] alongside an unknown number of research reports, conference presentations, working papers and so on. Although expenditure on research has been constrained in some countries since the financial crisis of 2008, there is no sign that the rates of increase in global research publications will fall in the foreseeable future.

Globalization and collaboration

In the context of these increases, there have been dramatic shifts in the global research landscape. Strong economic growth in countries such as Brazil, China and India has driven large increases in investment in R&D, which have in turn brought about huge rises in the volume of research outputs. Between 2006 and 2010, the annual growth rate in articles by authors from Brazil was 9.8%, from China 12.3% and from India 13.7%. Chinese authors accounted for 17.1% of the global total of articles published in 2010, and they are now second only to researchers in the USA in the number of articles published. Some countries starting from a lower base have seen even higher rates of growth: for Iran it was 25.2% between 2006 and 2010, for Malaysia 35.4%.[10] This global shift in the production of research outputs has been accompanied by a rise in international collaboration among researchers. Research is increasingly undertaken in a distributed and collaborative way that blurs the distinctions between countries, making it more difficult to attribute research inputs and outputs unequivocally to specific countries. But collaborations are increasingly focused in a core of countries (mainly from Western Europe and North America, but also including China and Japan) which collaborate with each other as well as with others on the periphery: collaborations in the periphery itself are relatively rare.

Research collaborations have been promoted by governments and other funders, who have encouraged researchers from different disciplines to come together to address large-scale research problems and issues – 'grand challenges' – that demand a wide range of approaches. Thus the Research Councils in the UK have for the past decade devoted considerable sums to cross-disciplinary research in areas such as (currently) global food security, lifelong health and well-being, and living with environmental change. Similar cross-disciplinary programmes of research have been promoted by the National Science Foundation and the National Academy of Engineering in the USA, while at an international level the International Council for Science has promoted the development of research in earth system science for global sustainability.

Research data

Both cross-disciplinary and international collaborations have been facilitated by developments in information and communications technologies. Many collaborations are conducted by researchers who rarely see each other in person. Computational and remote-sensing technologies have also created new ways of doing science. They have led to what some have referred to as a data deluge, and a new era of data-driven research, making use of huge collections of data created not only by researchers but also by a wide range of government, business and voluntary organizations. Linked data and Semantic Web technologies promise the creation of new information by deep integration of an increasing number of data sets of growing complexity, and new ways of reusing them. The Royal Society's report *Science as an Open Enterprise*[7] highlights the increasing importance of data in its own right as an output of research; and the increasing interest in how to help researchers to manage their data more effectively and to make it not only accessible but intelligible, assessable and usable by others to utilise in their own research and for other purposes. The report shows how the infrastructure and services through which data is made intelligently accessible and readily usable are now seen as essential for successful research. But we are far from that position: a generation ago most journal articles reported on findings relating to a relatively small number of data points, and it was relatively straightforward for researchers to present text and data in an integrated and informative way. Big data – and the analytics associated with it – has brought a growing gap between publications and data. John Wood and Henry Rzepa outline the opportunities associated with the use and the sharing of data, as well as some of the challenges if the important benefits are to be realized.

A key challenge for all concerned in the effective communication of research is therefore how to handle the increasingly complex relationships between books and articles, on the one hand, and, on the other, the data that underlies the findings that those publications present; and how to ensure that they are presented and made accessible together in an integrated way. Libraries and publishers, as well as specialist data centres, are playing an increasing part in developing cross-sectoral roles in helping to manage research data, and drafting policies to promote data sharing.

Most scholarly publishers accept that data and publications belong together. The relationship between them is sometimes presented as a pyramid with a broad base of raw data and data sets, on which researchers construct a smaller set of structured data collections and databases, then processed data and data representations, and topped off with the relatively small amount of data (typically in the form of small tables and charts) presented within the publication itself. Journal publishers increasingly link from articles to relevant data stored elsewhere, and some enable readers to interact with, and edit, data presented in the article itself. In the past five years journals have also seen a dramatic increase in the amount of supplementary material presented to them, along with articles in the traditional format. For some, this has become a growing problem, with the supplementary material exceeding in volume the articles themselves and presenting problems for peer review and quality assurance.

Publishers have an important role to play in making more of the data that researchers produce more readily available for others to scrutinize and reuse. Some are also enhancing articles to provide better integration with underlying data in the ways that Henry Rzepa discusses; ensuring that data has persistent identifiers to underpin effective two-way links between data and publications; and helping to promote guidelines for the proper citation of data. There is also scope for much more effective co-operation between publishers and data centres so as to facilitate integration between data and publications, including support for full interactivity when readers wish to reuse data; and for the publication of data journals that describe data sets and data methods. In an ideal world, journal articles would present text alongside seamless links, with interactive viewers, to relevant data sets. Consequently the quantity of supplementary material would fall. The availability of, and access to, publications and associated data would then become fully integrated in a creative and symbiotic relationship.

Publishers' changing roles

David Prosser discusses the two-way flow of influence between research and publishing; and the scale of the scholarly publishing industry is now remarkable. The value of the STM journal publishing business was estimated[11] to be $8.8 billion in 2009, with more than half the revenues being generated in the USA, c.30% in Europe, 10% in the Asia-Pacific region and 5% in the rest of the world. There are some two thousand publishers of scholarly journals across the world, publishing over 25,000 journals. About 8500 of them are indexed by Thomson-Reuters ISI database, and 16,500 in Elsevier's SCOPUS. The latest estimates suggest that over 1.9 million articles were published in these journals in 2010,[12] and that the number has been rising at around 3.5% a year.

Publishers range hugely in size and scope, and the distribution of journals between them is highly skewed:[13] the great majority publish only one or two journals, while the four largest – Elsevier, Wiley-Blackwell, Springer, and Taylor & Francis – have over a thousand each, including many that they publish on behalf of learned societies. Overall, the top 100 publishers are responsible for over two-thirds of all journals; and estimates suggest that commercial publishers are responsible for just under two-thirds of the articles published each year; learned societies for around 30%; and university presses and other publishers for the remainder. Journal titles, like publishers, vary hugely in size and scope, from the small niche journals that meet the needs of closely defined research and related communities, through the major disciplinary journals such as the *Journal of the American Chemical Society* or the *Journal of Fluid Mechanics*, to the major multi-disciplinary journals such as *Nature* and *Science*. Some titles publish hundreds or even thousands of articles each year; but many journals publish only 20 or fewer. It is notable also that journals have increased in size: between 1975 and 2001 the average number of articles in US science journals nearly doubled, from 85 to 154, while the average length of papers also increased over the same period, from 7.4 to 12.4 pages.[14]

While diversity remains a key characteristic, over the past decade there have been common threads in the experience of publishers and journals, and in their relationships with libraries and readers. We have now reached a position where the current contents – and in most cases the back-runs – of nearly all journal titles are available online. This has brought about a key shift in the relationship between libraries and publishers. Whereas libraries used to buy physical copies of journals, they now purchase licences under the terms of which publishers provide access to content held on their platforms.

The contents of journals are provided in PDF, as well as XML and HTML formats; and, as Richard Bennett and Henry Rzepa discuss, there are increasing moves towards the use of more sophisticated semantic mark-up with more extensive linking and interactive features that cannot easily be accommodated in PDFs. Publishers are also addressing the demands to make their content available on mobile devices including smartphones, tablets and e-book readers, where PDF formats are not appropriate. In this way they are responding to the growing demand for the content that they publish to be delivered through a range of devices, anywhere at any time.

Peer review

However the content is delivered, quality assurance through peer review is a key feature of what journals and publishers provide for both authors and readers. The principle of peer review – of subjecting authors' manuscripts to the scrutiny of experts in the field before publication – is widely seen as fundamental to the scholarly communications process.[15] The review process itself varies, but typically involves two or three reviewers as well as the editor of a journal, whose decision is final. To reduce the risk of bias, two main processes are used: single-blind review, in which the reviewers are aware of the authors' identities, but not vice versa; and double-blind review, in which neither party is aware of the other's identity. The former is more common, especially in the sciences; and there is evidence that in about half of double-blind review cases, reviewers can identify who the authors are. The results of the process may range from acceptance of the manuscript as it stands, through a requirement for relatively minor modifications, or substantial rewriting, or additional analysis or experimentation, to outright rejection.

The scholarly community is deeply committed to the principle of peer review, and recognizes the role that it plays in improving the quality of published papers. Researchers nevertheless accept that the practice of peer review is imperfect: on the one hand, it cannot provide guarantees against the publication of poor-quality, mistaken or even fraudulent research findings; and, on the other hand, there are risks that reviewers will fail to recognize work that is significant and important. The process brings with it inevitable delays in publication, not least because reviewers and editors devote considerable time to it. In a recent survey[16] authors reported average review times of around three months; and reviewers reported that they reviewed on average eight papers a year and spent five hours on each of them.

The role of publishers in peer review is to support the journal and the editor by managing the process – as Mike McGrath discusses in his very personal view of the relationship – with the help of online submission systems, which have brought faster publication times and reduced costs. Some systems also support editors and reviewers with automatic linking of references in authors' manuscripts; and many publishers are now also making use of the CrossCheck plagiarism detection system.[17] Despite these developments, however, there remains a strong feeling among many researchers that there is room for further improvements, especially to reduce the time taken, and the potential for biased reviews. There have thus been experiments in completely open peer review, in which not only the identities of reviewers and authors are disclosed but also the content of reviews; and in some cases the reviews are presented to readers alongside the published paper. Some OA publishers, such as PLoS, are also experimenting with post-publication review, seeking to exploit the 'wisdom of the crowd' by allowing readers to review and comment on papers online, and to rate them on a numerical scale following publication. The experiments have not been wholly successful: researchers seem reluctant to participate, perhaps because they fear the possible consequences of being identified as the source of negative reviews, comments or ratings.

Given the importance attached to peer review, it is perhaps surprising that there is relatively little systematic information available about its effectiveness: rates of acceptance and rejection across ranges of journals and disciplines; the rates at which modifications are recommended or required; or the extents to which authors cascade their submissions from one journal to another or revise their submissions as a result of the peer review process. There is similarly little systematic information about the success of peer review in detecting fraudulent or faulty research findings. Anecdotal evidence suggests that the number of corrections to, and retractions of, papers has been rising in recent years, but it is not clear whether this is the result of improved post-publication checks or of increases in the numbers and proportion of sub-standard papers. There is clearly room for research in all these areas.

Big Deals

A key change arising from electronic publishing has been the rise of bundles and Big Deals. The number of journals sold on the basis of individual subscriptions has fallen sharply, and it has been estimated that over half of all journals are now sold in bundles of 50 titles or more.[18] Nearly all large and most medium-sized publishers offer bundles of content, often including not only journals but also e-books, reference works and data sets. And smaller publishers can participate in multi-publisher bundles such as those provided by BioOne or Project MUSE. The result has been a huge increase in the number of journal titles accessible through university libraries; and Roger Schonfeld discusses how library users have embraced the change.

But the pricing of Big Deals is complex: for while the price of individual titles is discounted deeply, publishers are in effect expanding their market by shifting libraries from highly selective to larger, all-encompassing collections. Most publishers still price bundles on the basis of the 'prior print' model, where they provide libraries with electronic access to all the titles in the bundle at a price reflecting the library's previous print subscriptions plus a top-up fee for electronic-only access to titles that were not subscribed to in the past.[19] How much longer such a pricing model is sustainable is clearly open to question. But other pricing models – whether based on levels of usage, on institutional size or on the numbers of simultaneous users – pose problems too, and the transition from one model to another inevitably gives rise to anomalies. A key issue for libraries is the extent to which publishers allow cancellations of titles during the term of the licence, which is typically for three years or more; this is becoming a bigger problem as libraries face increasing financial pressure, and the need to scrutinize their acquisition budgets ever more stringently.

Open Access

Financial pressures, along with increasing awareness of the potential offered by new technologies and services, and changing expectations about the availability of content on the internet, have together added momentum to the OA movement. For there is a growing perception across the world we have not yet realized the full potential of the online environment for providing access to scholarly publications. Hence there is increasing interest not only in the compelling principle that the results of publicly funded research should be freely accessible in the public domain but also in how to ensure that the principle is applied in practice. There is a strong case to be made that removing restrictions on the flows into society and the economy of the information and knowledge that researchers produce will bring a number of benefits, as outlined by Robert Kiley.

Open Access journals

The number of OA journals has risen rapidly since they first began to emerge in the 1990s. As of the summer of 2012, over 8000 OA journals were listed in the Directory of Open Access Journals (DOAJ, www.doaj.org), published in 117 countries, with the USA (1231), Brazil (753) and the UK (546) at the head of the list. Some have questioned the DOAJ statistics, but it is clear that OA journals now represent a significant and growing proportion of the journals published globally. Most are relatively new, and have been OA from the start, many of them founded by individual scholars on tailor-made platforms, often with a business model based on voluntary labour and the free use of a university's web server. Others are older established journals that have converted to OA; while new OA publishers such as BioMedCentral and PLoS have established a large-scale presence in the market, funding themselves by charging article-publishing charges (APCs) before publication.

In addition to the fully OA journals, nearly all the large scholarly publishers now operate at least some of their journals on a hybrid model: that is, in return for the payment of an APC, they will make an article in an otherwise subscription-based journal accessible immediately on publication, without any subscription or pay-per-view charges.

The proportion of the global total of articles published each year in OA or hybrid journals is not easy to calculate. It has been estimated that over 190,000 articles were published in OA journals in 2009,[20] about 7.7% of all peer-reviewed journal articles published that year. The EU-funded Study of Open Access Publishing (SOAP: http://project-soap.eu) estimated that a slightly higher 8–10% of all peer-reviewed articles were published OA. Such figures should be set in context: the total number of articles in all kinds of peer-reviewed journals worldwide is rising at around 3.5% a year.

Most publishers providing fully OA journals operate on a small scale, with only one title, and publish fewer than 100 articles a year. A recent study[21] suggests that two-thirds of OA articles are published by 10% of publishers, and that 14 publishers are responsible for around 30% of all OA articles. Science, technology and medicine account for two-thirds of journals, and more than three-quarters of articles. Social science and humanities, on the other hand, account for a third of journals, but only 16% of articles.

Take-up of the OA option in hybrid journals is still relatively low, at around 2% on average. Some publishers have seen higher take-up levels in certain disciplines: at Oxford Journals 10% of authors in the life sciences select the OA option across 16 journals, as against approximately 5% in medicine and public health and 3% in the humanities and social sciences. Nature Communications, on the other hand, reports take-up of the OA option at over 40%.

Overall, recent studies suggest that OA articles are growing in number much faster than the 3.5% a year seen for all published articles. This is the result both of the creation of new 'born OA' journals and of the switch of established journals either to OA or to the hybrid model. The recent development of what have been termed 'repository' journals, such as *PLoSOne* – where the peer-review process focuses solely on whether the findings and conclusions are justified by the results and methodology presented, rather than on assessment of the relative importance of the research or perceived level of interest it will generate – has stimulated further growth. Established publishers such as American Institute of Physics, Nature Publishing Group, the BMJ (British Medical Journal) Group and SAGE Publications in the social sciences have all launched similar journals in the past couple of years. *PLoSOne* is now by most counts the biggest journal in the world. Such journals play a role different from the highly selective journals which seek to present only the best and most significant research in their fields. But it seems likely that repository journals – and indeed the whole group of OA and hybrid journals – will continue to grow. Following the Finch Report and the acceptance of its recommendations, that growth will be stimulated in the UK by the Research Councils' providing – like the Wellcome Trust – more straightforward mechanisms for the funding of APCs than they have done up to now.

New OA journals have been launched recently both by established publishers – such as Nature Publishing Group, Wiley-Blackwell and Springer – and also by new journals such as *PeerJ* (https://peerj.com), co-founded by Peter Binfield (formerly at *PLoSOne*) and Jason Hoyt (formerly at Mendeley) with financial backing from O'Reilly Media, and *eLife* (www.elifesciences.org), a new journal published jointly by the Howard Hughes Medical Institute, the Max Planck Society and the Wellcome Trust. And SCOAP3 (http://scoap3.org), an international consortium of institutions engaged in high-energy physics, has recently invited tenders for OA publishing in its subject domain.

Repositories

Open access repositories have also become an increasingly familiar part of the landscape. There are now, according to the Directory of Open Access Repositories (www.opendoar.org) over two thousand worldwide, the great majority based in universities or other research institutions. They vary hugely in size and scope; in the kinds of records they contain (many include reports and working papers, conference papers and posters, dissertations and theses, designs, exhibition materials, performances and so on, as well as published papers); and in the amount of material that they make available in full text, as distinct from simply metadata records. In many of the larger institutional repositories, the majority of items are recorded only as metadata.

Universities and other research institutions have established repositories for many different reasons: providing showcases for their research, on the one hand, and establishing central records of their research outputs (not least for assessment purposes), on the other. As Mark Brown notes, libraries have played a key part in setting up and running repositories; but patterns of deposit and use remain patchy.

The largest institutional repository in the UK, for example, is the University College London (UCL) Discovery repository (http://discovery.ucl.ac.uk), with over 225,000 items. It contains a wide array of reports, posters, working papers, theses, conference presentations, designs, exhibition materials, performances and the like, in addition to journal articles. But while journal articles constitute the larger part of its content (more than 70% of the total), the great majority – 98% – consists of metadata records only: as of 31 July 2012, the UCL repository included only 2134 full-text articles, of which 197 were published in 2010 and 112 in 2011. Similar patterns can be seen across many other institutional repositories, both in the UK and across the world: the DASH repository at Harvard (http://dash.harvard.edu) provides access to only a small proportion of the publications produced by Harvard faculty.

It is difficult at present to get consolidated or detailed information on levels of usage of the material in institutional repositories. Some of the larger ones record impressive levels of downloads, but patterns of usage tend to focus on unpublished material: at UCL, only nine of the top 50 items downloaded in 2011 were published journal articles (and they tended to be relatively old: the top two articles were published in 2001 and 2002, respectively).

For researchers in certain disciplines, however, subject-based repositories are an important part of their environment: a place to find information, to see what's new, to share early findings with their peers and to look for collaborators, as well as to deposit their own articles. Provision is very patchy, and there are many gaps; but services such as arXiv – predominantly but not solely for the physics community – have gained a prominent position in the daily workflows of researchers, as have CiteSeer in computer and information science and PubMedCentral in biomedical and life sciences.

- ArXiv (http://arxiv.org) is a preprint repository, with c.735,000 full-text articles, growing at about 75,000 articles a year, and about 1 million downloads a week. There is relatively light filtering of incoming papers for quality-control purposes; but most papers are subsequently submitted to a journal such as *Physical Review Letters* for peer review and publication.
- CiteSeer (http://citeseerx.ist.psu.edu) harvests documents and other material such as algorithms, data, metadata, services, techniques and software; and it creates a citation index to facilitate literature search and evaluation. It has over 1.5 million documents, with nearly 1.5 million unique authors and 30 million citations.
- PubMedCentral (PMC, www.ncbi.nlm.nih.gov/pmc) is an online archive of biomedical journal articles developed by the US National Library of Medicine (NLM) as one of the key measures to support

the National Institutes of Health's (NIH) policy to make all the research it funds freely accessible to anyone. It currently contains 2.4 million full-text articles, growing at a rate of about 10% a year. Most PMC articles have a corresponding entry in PubMed, the database of citations and abstracts which provides links to full-text articles at journal websites. UKPMC (http://ukpmc.ac.uk) established a partnership with PMC in 2007. In addition to access to most of the content in PMC itself, it provides a manuscript-submission system for publishers and researchers to submit articles for inclusion in the UKPMC collection, along with information about researchers and research grants. Free access to the material in it is mandatory, but publishers can delay release of their material for up to 12 months. Over 35,000 articles have been deposited in UKPMC since it was established, the great majority by publishers; and 200,000 visits (5000 searches) are made to it each day.

But while repositories like these have become an essential part of the working environment for researchers in their disciplines and subject areas, researchers in many other fields lack the benefits that can come from repositories that have a sufficient critical mass of material to be truly effective.

In sum, while there is a fairly comprehensive set of institutional repositories, in many countries, including the UK, rates of deposit and usage of published materials remain low; and it is still not clear whether they can fulfil a bigger and more effective role in providing quick and ready access to research publications for the longer term. Repositories may remain important in the years ahead as showcases for the research activities and outputs of their host institutions and as links with research management systems, and also as mechanisms for preserving and providing access to research findings and outputs not formally published, including research data, working papers, technical specifications and reports, theses and dissertations. It seems likely, however, that those subject-based repositories that have already reached a significant scale – such that researchers in the relevant fields and disciplines cannot ignore them – will continue to evolve. This in turn may encourage the development of similar services in other subject areas.

Developing the service infrastructure

Publishers, libraries, aggregators and others, including the general search engines such as Google, have invested heavily to make it easy for researchers and others to discover and navigate the huge volumes of research content now available online. Readers can thus discover and gain access to such content through a wide range of 'gateway' services, as well as through publisher platforms; and services such as citation linking and chaining are underpinned by the allocation of persistent identifiers (in the form of digital object identifiers [DOIs]) managed by CrossRef (www.crossref.org).

These developments have been accompanied by huge investment in systems to manage the flows of information along the various supply chains: between authors, publishers, aggregators, subscription agents, libraries and end-users. Developing systems and standards to facilitate effective and more open flows of metadata continues to be the focus of much effort, along with systems to generate consistent and more sophisticated information about users and usage. Licensing has also required considerable investment in systems to manage access: libraries and publishers have jointly established elegant systems to authenticate and authorize users so that they can gain access to the published content that they are entitled to read, and to try to ensure that they are not denied access free at the point of use when that is indeed what they are entitled to.

The infrastructure of citation, indexing and navigation services such as Thomson Reuters' ISI Web of Knowledge (http://wokinfo.com/) and Elsevier's SCOPUS[22] has also seen important developments. These services provide bibliographic records and related content, along with the tools to search, access, analyse and manage published research information of various kinds and to make it easy to explore specialized fields within a discipline or across disciplines. Citation indexing makes it possible to track from one publication to another, to identify the papers with the greatest impact in a field and to determine key influences, patterns and trends in research. The scope of the literature covered, and the power and sophistication of the available tools, have increased hugely in recent years. Bibliometrics, scientometrics and webometrics are becoming increasingly important in analysing, measuring and assessing research outputs and performance; and their influence seems likely to increase further.

Data and analytics

Such developments are set in a wider context, with stakeholders getting to grips with the complexities and the potential of big data, linked data and data analytics. Recently some publishers – stimulated in part by experimentation from members of the research community – have started to use web and Semantic Web technologies to enhance journal articles in ways which some have termed 'semantic publishing'. This has included enriching the text by providing interactive figures and 'semantic lenses', which turn a table into a graph or animate a diagram; providing links to definitions of terms or concepts, or to additional information about such terms, or about relevant people or organizations; direct links to all cited references; access to the data within the article in actionable form, and links to the full data sets that underlie the article; and machine-readable metadata. The aim of enriching articles in such ways is to make the content easier to discover, analyse, extract, combine and reuse.

Meanwhile there is increasing interest in exploiting the potential of text-mining tools to analyse and process the information contained in collections or corpora of journal articles and other documents in order to extract and manipulate information, and to generate new information. The use of such techniques is not yet widespread, not least because arrangements for making publications available for text mining can be complex, and because the entry costs are high for those who lack the necessary technical skills. But text mining offers considerable potential to increase the efficiency, effectiveness and quality of research, to unlock hidden information, and to develop new knowledge. In the UK, the government has accepted a proposal in the Hargreaves report[23] to remove one of the barriers to wider adoption of text mining by creating a copyright exception to cover text and data analytics for non-commercial research within restricted limits. This would allow whole copyright works to be copied for the purposes of text mining and data mining for non-commercial research.[24] Some publishers are concerned about the practicalities of such an exception and about the risks of text-mined material being made available to third parties for reuse. Nonetheless it seems clear that text mining will become more prominent over the next few years.

Co-operation and innovation

It is important to provide incentives for all players in the scholarly communications landscape – and for new entrants – to continue to experiment and innovate. There are signs, for example, that initiatives from both established and newer organizations are beginning to make a significant impact on how researchers in the UK and beyond discover, gain access to, use and manage the published resources relevant to their work. Major publishers – subscription based and OA – are transforming the ways in which articles are presented online, with ever more sophisticated links and interactive features. Many publishers, libraries and other intermediaries are developing systems to enable them to analyse patterns of usage and impact more deeply; and to present them to their users.

Established players are also working together with new ones – such as Mendeley (www.mendeley.com) and Zotero (www.zotero.org) – who are developing new services to help researchers to gather, organize and analyse published and unpublished resources more effectively, to manage their workflows and to collaborate and share their work with others. There is continued experimentation with user ratings and comments, and the development of 'alt-metrics' that measure impact based on readership and reuse indicators gathered from social media and collaborative annotation tools. The sharing of such metrics can act as a filter for alerting readers to material that may be relevant and important to their work, and in some ways can serve as another mechanism of peer review.

National and academic research libraries are also working together, as Mark Brown discusses, to develop the service infrastructure not just in areas such as search and navigation, but also in long-term curation and preservation. These issues have become much more complex in the digital and online environments, where libraries themselves often do not control scholarly content as they did in the print and manuscript world. Digitization of analogue content has played a huge role in making material accessible to untold numbers of people who would in the past not have been able to consult it in libraries and archives. But the curation and preservation of digital content demands collaboration at local, national and international levels between researchers, libraries and publishers. So far, libraries have tended to take the lead on this. But there is some way to go before we have clear and robust systems and procedures in place to ensure that all the publications and other valuable material produced by researchers – sometimes referred to as the 'minutes of science' – are preserved for the long term.

The infrastructure of services is, in these various ways, continuing to change rapidly. Some researchers and other commentators go so far as to suggest that scientific journals have outlived their usefulness, that pre-publication peer review is a broken mechanism, that packaging and marketing articles in journals is pointless and that the quest for prestige by publishing in high-status journals is harmful. In the online world, they suggest, there is no need for journals to disseminate research results: all that is needed is a website. In this view, the whole infrastructure of services built up by libraries, publishers and others no longer serves any useful purpose; rather, it imposes needless costs and constraints and reduces the flow of knowledge that researchers create. Scholars should simply make their findings available, and let their peers decide on their veracity and value. Whether that is likely to become the norm any time soon is not yet clear.

Conclusion

> If manure be suffered to lie in idle heaps, it breeds stink and vermin. If properly diffused, it vivifies and fertilizes. The same is true of capital and knowledge. A monopoly of either breeds filth and abomination. A proper diffusion of them fills a country with joy and endurance.
>
> (*Poor Man's Guardian*, 1834)

The systems and processes of scholarly communication have undergone profound and disruptive change in the last decade: changes in the roles of the key agents in the system – researchers, universities, libraries, funders, publishers, secondary publishers and other service providers; changes in how they fulfil those roles; changes in the relationships between the key agents; and changes in the behaviours and expectations not just of researchers – in their roles as both producers and consumers – but of a wide range of other people and organizations who are interested in research and its results. What has not changed is the fundamental purpose of research and communication: generating and disseminating new knowledge. The need for more and better fertilizer endures; so does the need for better and speedier ways of spreading it.

References

1 Working Group on Expanding Access to Published Research Findings (2012) *Accessibility, Sustainability, Excellence: how to expand access to research publications*, London.

2 Department for Business Innovation and Skills (2012) *Letter to Dame Janet Finch on the Government Response to the Finch Group Report: 'Accessibility, sustainability, excellence: how to expand access to research publications'*, London.

3 Research Councils UK (2012) *Policy on Access to Research Outputs* (July), www.rcuk.ac.uk/documents/documents/RCUK%20_Policy_on_Access_ to_Research_Outputs.pdf.

4 European Commission (2012) *Towards Better Access to Scientific Information: boosting the benefits of public investments in research*, COM(2012) 401, Brussels.

5 European Commission (2012) *Recommendation on Access to and Preservation of Scientific Information*, C(2012) 4890 final, Brussels.

6 Office of Science and Technology Policy (2013) *Memorandum for the Heads of Executive Departments and Agencies: Increasing access to the results of federal funded scientific research*, Washington, DC.

7 Royal Society (2012) *Science as an Open Enterprise*, London.

8 See OECD, *Science and Technology Main Indicators*, www.oecd.org/sti/scienceandtechnologypolicy/ mainscienceandtechnologyindicatorsmsti20122edition.htm.

9 National Science Board (2012) *Science and Engineering Indicators 2012* (NSB 12-01), Arlington, VA.

10 Elsevier (2011) *International Comparative Performance of the UK Research Base 2011: report for the Department of Business, Innovation and Skills*, London.

11 Outsell, *Information Industry Market Size and Share Rankings: preliminary 2008 results*, www.outsellinc.com/store/products/795.

12 Ware, M. and Mabe, M. (2009) *The STM Report: an overview of scientific and scholarly journals publishing*, International Association of Scientific, Technical and Medical Publishers.

13 King, D. W. (2007) The Cost of Journal Publishing: a literature review and commentary, *Learned Publishing*, **20**, 85–106.

14 Hames, I. (2007) *Peer Review and Manuscript Management in Scientific Journals*, Blackwell Publishing in Association with ALPSP.

15 Research Information Network (2010) *Peer Review, A Guide for Researchers*, London.

16 Ware, M. (2008) *Peer Review: benefits, perceptions and alternatives*, Publishing

Research Consortium.

17 www.crossref.org/crosscheck/index.html.

18 Van Orsdel, L. C. and Born, K. (2009) In the Face of the Downturn, Libraries and Publishers Brace for Big Cuts, *Library Journal*, www.libraryjournal.com/article/CA6651248.html.

19 Cox, J. and Cox, L. (2008) *Academic Journal Publishers' Policies and Practices in Online Publishing*, 3rd edn, ALPSP.

20 Laakso, M., et al. (2010) The Development of OA Journal Publishing 1993–2009, *PLoS ONE*, **6** (6).

21 Dallmeier-Tiessen, S. et al. (2010) *First Results of the SOAP Project: Open Access publishing in 2010*, http://arxiv.org/ftp/arxiv/papers/1010/1010.0506.pdf.

22 www.scopus.com/scopus/home.url.

23 Hargreaves, I. (2011) *Digital Opportunity: a review of intellectual property and growth*, Intellectual Property Office.

24 *Modernising Copyright: a modern, robust and flexible framework. Government response to consultation on copyright exceptions and clarifying copyright law*, Intellectual Copyright Office, 2012.

Part 1
Changing researcher behaviour

1

Changing ways of sharing research in chemistry

Henry S. Rzepa

ABSTRACT

The challenges of sharing research in chemistry are introduced via the molecule and how its essential information features might be formalized. The review then covers a period of around 33 years, describing how scientists used to share information about the molecule, and how that sharing has evolved during a period that has seen the widespread introduction of several disruptive technologies. These include e-mail and its now ubiquitous attachment, the world wide web and its modern expression via blogs and wikis. The review describes how digital documents have similarly evolved during this period, acquiring in some cases digital rights management, metadata and most recently an existence in the cloud. The review also describes how the dissemination of digital research data has also changed dramatically, the most recent innovation being data repositories, and speculates what the future of sharing research via the latest disruptive technology, tablets, might be.

Introduction

Chemistry is widely considered to stand at the crossroads of many disciplines, with signposts to molecular, life, materials, polymer, environmental and computer sciences, as well as to physics and mathematics, and even art and design. To collaborate and share research data and ideas across these areas, research scientists must strive (and do not always succeed) to find common languages to express their intended concepts. In reality, even different scientific dialects can be a challenge, since the semantics of multi-disciplinary areas of research are rarely defined accurately or fully enough for people to cope with the ambiguities and subtleties. The modern digital information age has promised a revolutionary approach to these challenges, the latest incarnations being the formation of social networks to facilitate the interaction. This chapter will present a perspective on some of these aspects from my personal point of view as a research chemist. There are many crossroads at which one could stand: I can only follow the sage advice of Yogi Berra: 'When one comes to a fork in the road one should take it'![1] Here I will take the fork to molecular sciences.

My starting-point is a molecule. There are about 65 million[2] that have been formally shared by scientists (and quite a few more that may not have been shared). How do we know this? Well, in the mid-19th century an enlightened scientist called Konrad Beilstein decided to create a molecular taxonomy. Far fewer molecules were known then, of course, but he had the vision to realize that their number was going to grow, very probably exponentially. This was because more and more chemists were sharing 'recipes' or protocols for producing new molecules and developing ways of describing the properties of the new entrants. Beilstein's taxonomic project was based on three steps:

1   identify a new molecule
2   classify its measured structural characteristics and properties
3   identify the researcher(s) who reported these properties (what we now know as a literature citation).

Nowadays, almost all aspects of this project are conducted with the help of digital tools. The first task is to formally convert the structure of a new molecule into a digital expression. This expression is called a *connection table* and attempts to define which atoms in any molecule are connected to other atoms in the same molecule. The molecule may in fact also comprise several components unconnected by bonds but nevertheless inseparable. It soon became clear that molecular scientists needed to define more carefully what they meant by a connection; and in fact they came to call this a (chemical) *bond*. It sounds simple enough: all that molecular scientists need to do is agree among themselves what a bond is. The first person to attempt this in modern terms was G. N. Lewis, in a famous article published in 1916[3] outlining how a bond could be defined in terms of shared electrons. The development of quantum mechanics in the 1920s allowed these apparently simple definitions to be formalized mathematically, and physics played its part by showing how X-ray crystallography might provide experimental measurement of such bonds. There are of course grey areas, especially nowadays when odder and odder bonds are continually being discovered and require constant refinement of the definitions of a bond. But by the time that the modern digital era started in the 1960s, connection tables for essentially all new molecules could be produced. The task was so gargantuan, however, that only a small number of commercial organizations could afford the resources (mostly human at that stage) to do this.

Armed with a connection table, a research scientist was in a position to contemplate formulating a search for a specific molecule about which others had shared information. Until around 1979, scientists had to visit in person what was often the one library at their organization with the shelf space to store the collected chemical indices, and systematically hunt through each five-year volume on the basis of a systematic name. That name was derived from the connection table, and part of the chemist's skill was the ability to infer such names from a set of rules acquired during training. From my own experience, I can vouch that it would take around five hours to find research information on a molecule such as that represented (in two dimensions) in Figure 1.1. In reality, even for a relatively simple system, deriving its systematic name was often too great a challenge. Instead, the community would refer to it by what was known as a trivial name, information to be acquired by (sometimes serendipitous)

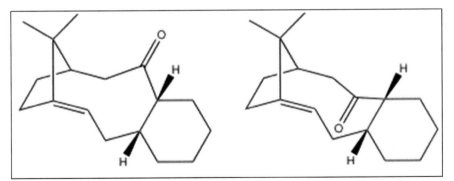

Figure 1.1 A molecule (and a stereoisomer) represented by a connection table, indicated by lines representing bonds

reading of books and articles, or indeed by talking to colleagues. And it would be difficult to stray too far from one's own specialist area.

However, from 1979 onwards access to such world collections of molecules started to go online, and an institution's library could now be expected to offer an online searching service. This involved booking an appointment with a specialist librarian (with around two weeks' notice, due to heavy demand). The librarian would be trained to understand how to formulate the required search syntax in such a diagram. For the first time, the scientist could realistically expect to search all the information on known molecules, rather than just the small subset determined by the amount of time he had available. Moreover, he could formulate a search based on a degree of similarity, rather than on exact matches, and so be far more adventurous in his searches.

At this stage a molecular query was formulated in terms of integer connectivity, such as $1 =$ a bond connection (mapping to one line in the above diagram) and $0 =$ pairs of atoms with no such connection. For many scientists, this description seemed too restrictive, and so in the early 1970s a project was initiated to collect and share the experimental data from which the bond connectivity could be quantified as a length. This initiative became in time the Cambridge Crystallographic Data Centre, which nowadays disseminates information on around 600,000 molecules on a commercial basis. It provides accurate 3D co-ordinates for all the atoms in a molecule, which allows much richer information about them to be inferred. I use the word *disseminates*, which does not mean quite the same as *shares*. The distinction relates to the difference between open and closed sharing of research, to which I shall return several times in this chapter.

By the early 1980s a more general scientific online presence was emerging, and central libraries no longer held the monopoly of access points to such information. Indeed a typical researcher might have one access point in his own building, maybe even reasonably near his office. In 1985 we reached another important fork in the road. Most individual researchers now regarded the software tools to describe molecules digitally as essential. This opened up a new paradigm for sharing chemistry. The date is quite specific, since it corresponds to the introduction of the Macintosh personal computer and two of the tools, in particular, that appealed to visually oriented chemists (including those who had difficulty naming molecules, see below). The first was a mouse-driven sketching tool that could be used to represent the molecular connection table pictorially (and is still used to this day to draft diagrams such as shown in Figure 1.1). The second was the ability to transmit the diagram to a high-quality laser printer via a computer network. This network was built so that the cost of the printer (in those days a more expensive resource than the personal computer itself) could be shared among many researchers.[4] Although few realized the significance at the time, a spin-out benefit of the creation of such a network enabled something far more world changing than simply connecting a computer to a printer. Adding a so-called network router to the system also enabled an individual user's computer to be connected (via the somewhat unlikely printer port) to two new resources for sharing: e-mail and the then nascent internet. This in turn introduced researchers to entirely new paradigms for sharing their research and collaborating with others. A pictorial representation of the molecule (the natural language that had developed following Lewis's definition of the bond, see Figure 1.1) could now be immediately shared with any other researcher in the world with access to similar resources – admittedly in 1985 not very many. I say immediately, because the process involving the conventional, journal-based way of sharing was at that time often taking two years from start to finish, hardly an immediate process.

There was still another problem to be resolved: how to share the underlying data used to generate that picture. While e-mail was starting to allow two or more people to exchange information without delay, it was not yet recognized that reuse in a machine/software sense was also desirable.

E-mail as a content delivery mechanism for sharing research

E-mail became an increasingly popular tool for most scientists from 1985 onwards. This is significant because it introduced two components for dialogue: a loosely structured natural-language discourse and the document *attachment* facility associated with the process. The latter was a way of 'shrink wrapping' research ideas based in a standard document format, and particularly of the research data underpinning the ideas. Defined by a standard specification called the MIME type, it allowed a labelling of the document to ensure that the recipient's e-mail program could correctly process what it received.[5] In fact, this allowed the research scientist (in principle anyway) to share his research data with others in a manner that would allow the recipient to invoke the appropriate software so as to add further layers of semantic meaning to the received data and information. In practice, this feature was never fully exploited with e-mail: to this day the MIME label is used to 'wrap' a relatively limited set of document types, such as word-processed files, numerical spreadsheets, graphic images and a format known as PDF or portable document format, itself a spin-out from the Postscript printer description introduced with the first laser printers.

Chemists (especially those whose activity centred on molecules) would more often than not share their research by simply sending an attachment comprising a chemical document to others. The recipient still had to put in informed effort to ensure the attachment was compatible with his particular computer and software. The document itself normally ended up in a non-hierarchical folder called 'attachments', with little information about its content available, because senders were not constrained by any particular naming convention for the file name. The 'metadata' describing these e-mail attachments are sparse (once they are ensconced in the attachments folder, their association with the MIME type is lost). The process of rescuing such information has been memorably described by scientists as *defrosting the digital library*.[6]

The web as a content-delivery mechanism for sharing research

The document deluge was about to be greatly increased by the next wave of mechanisms for sharing research. Starting in 1994, most of the world's scientific research publications and journals undertook a gradual journey online, promoted largely by the exponential adoption of the system known as the world wide web.[7] From the outset, it was apparent that this mechanism had rather different attributes, as compared with e-mail, for sharing information and data.

1 Whereas e-mail was a 'push' mechanism initiated by the content holder, the web was a 'pull' mechanism initiated by the content requester (which could be either a human or a software agent). The difference is subtle but important, in that it led directly to the era of the search engine.

2 The pull request was made using a standard known as a uniform resource locator (URL), a now familiar term.

3 Although URL itself was standard, it soon proved not to be permanent over a time-scale of years/decades. A mechanism known generically as a 'handle' was introduced to solve this problem. The handle system[8] was designed as a more permanent mechanism to identify a document, with the handle being resolved into a URL at the time of the request. The best-known implementation of such handle resolution is the DOI (digital object identifier).[9] Since 2005, virtually all publishers of scientific journals have fully implemented this mechanism (at the time of writing, 52,678,814 DOIs had been assigned).[10]

4 As a result of the wide adoption of these standards, researchers now tend to exchange these DOI identifiers between themselves, citing them in e-mails, in documents (both word processing and PDF), in web pages and embedded in other recent expressions of web pages such as blog, wikis and podcasts (see below).

5 Although most web-based journal articles may ubiquitously have an associated DOI, the naming conventions used for the DOI itself tend to be publisher-specific, often inscrutable, and in themselves tell little about the content of the article. Many documents, particularly those not associated with collaborating publishers, do not have such a unique handle.

6 In 1994 it was recognized that the MIME mechanism, already matured in the e-mail environment, could also help to identify the context of a web-based document. In the area of chemistry, specifically, a Chemical MIME label was introduced.[5] Some 50 types of chemical document were identified, a taxonomy that helped to define the types of data available to chemists.

These mechanisms allowed documents to be linked into web pages, and shared with chemists in a reusable manner. This concept introduced a differentiation between *discourse*, of which the prime carrier was the journal article, and *data*, which itself could be contained in a document associated with a MIME type. The former was focused on the human reader, while the latter had a structured and standard form intended to be reused in conjunction with computer software. The latter could be used to transform the data into a visual representation to help scientists in their quantitative assessment of their models and associated interpretation, or as the input into further numerical analysis and model building.

The document type as a container for shared research

As the web was becoming established as the pre-eminent mechanism for delivering journal articles to their readers, so the wrapper for that content settled down into two principal digital formats. First, the portable document format or PDF (nowadays also generically referred to by the proprietary name Acrobat) represented essentially a printable version, which in appearance emulated the traditional look and feel of the bound journal article, complete with pagination, headers and footers. We might describe this as a format where the content and its style of presentation, its look and feel, are tightly integrated into a sealed and largely tamper-proof container.

While the full text could now be digitally searched within the PDF document, it was not designed as an innovative format departing radically from its heritage of the printable page. One exception to this, of potential interest in the molecular sciences, was the introduction of a 3D enhancement to Acrobat. This allowed models containing 3D model co-ordinates to be embedded into the document. This, in turn, enabled interactive rotation in order to change the viewing angle of the object. Creating such documents is complex, and few scientists have chosen to share their research in this manner to date.[11] Moreover, this could be also regarded as a limitation to sharing since the model contains no accessible (structured) underlying data. In other words, it is a passive object suitable only for viewing by a human, but not for reprocessing or reusing in the manner appropriate for a scientific investigation.

Second, in parallel with the PDF document, research could also be shared by the publisher through the adoption of an HTML presentational format. Most journals offer both formats for their readers. In practice, the

HTML is generated automatically by a production workflow originating from a word-processor document and the original authors have little participation in its generation. Although in principle HTML, as a mark-up language, offers a non-proprietary and interactively rich environment for sharing research, the lack of author involvement in its preparation has limited the 'added value' of this mode of presentation. However, I would argue that more general mark-up languages have much, as yet unexploited, potential for enhancing the sharing of research.[12] The basis for this assertion is a series of experiments that we undertook to demonstrate this.[13] Figure 1.2 is just one example of such enhancement.

Of course you are viewing this figure in black and white, statically on the pages of a book: the original is in colour and fully rotatable and interactive. At the bottom, the original caption contains hyperlinks to scripts adding annotations in the form of measurements of a 3D object (a portion of the DNA molecule, in this example) or links to additional data. Such 'added value' can be accessed only through the original journal

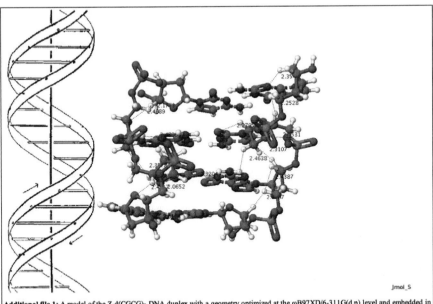

Additional file 1: A model of the Z-d(CGCG)$_2$ DNA duplex with a geometry optimized at the ωB97XD/6-311G(d,p) level and embedded in a continuum solvent field for water. (a) Load coordinates for Z-d(CGCG)2 and (b) measure for close van der Waals contacts or (c) O...C contacts. (d) Load coordinates for the diastereomeric B-d(CGCG)2 and (e) view the O...H-N and C-H...O close contacts. (f) Load Z-d(ATAT)2 and (g) view the close O...C contacts. (h) Load B-d(ATAT)2 and (i) view the close O...H-N contacts.

Figure 1.2 An example of an enhanced figure as part of a scientific article. The diagram is fully rotatable and interactive

page. Unlike with an Acrobat 3D object, the user also has access to this data in the mode illustrated in Figure 1.3 and thus has a portal into further research exploration.

Such enhanced attributes of a journal article, however, raise an important new issue. Conventionally, most scientists and chemists are assumed to be familiar with a fairly standard set of tools that they use to share their research: a word processor and (for, e.g., chemists) the chemical structure drawing program (see Figure 1.1). These tools are, however, limited when it comes to handling the data that is so essential for enhancing an article in the manner shown in Figures 1.2 and 1.3. Few authors acquire the necessary skills, and it might be said that few have the motivation needed to handle such data. It may also transpire that incorporating enhancements such as are shown in Figure 1.2 into the journal production workflow might in turn result in greatly increased costs to both the author and the institutional library, in the form of increased

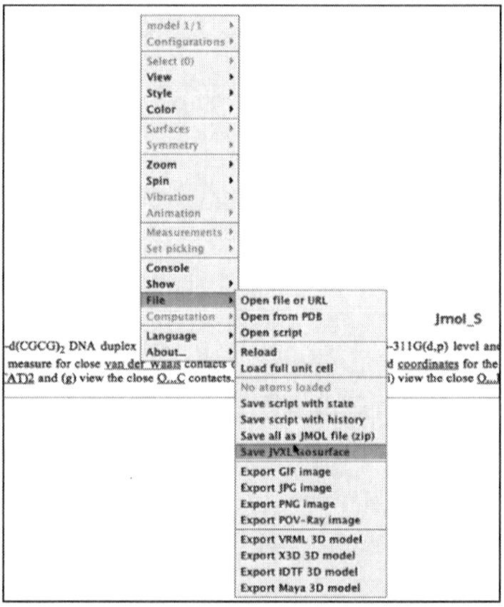

Figure 1.3 An illustration of how research data can be extracted from an enhanced journal figure

subscription charges. We may get a glimpse of this in how many publishers already surcharge authors for incorporating colour plates into their discourse, or for making an article available via an Open Access (OA) licence. The article from which Figure 1.2 is derived is OA, and that in turn allows me to include a representation of it in this chapter.

The need for interactivity has, however, emerged from a different direction. Around 2005, electronic books, or e-books, started to have a significant commercial impact. Devices such as the Amazon Kindle or the Apple iPad began to demonstrate how portable electronic access to bookstores can transform a market. Although both devices come with their own proprietary format, a more open format, known as *epub* has also emerged.[14] This is in fact nothing more than the aforementioned HTML wrapped into a compressed bundle and described by a manifest. The latest specification, epub3, adds the element of interactivity possible with, for example, Figure 1.2, and this in turn is based on the latest HTML standard, known as HTML5.[15] Even the presentation of the conventional static diagram is evolving. Images and diagrams are traditionally included in HTML documents, using bit-mapped formats such as JPG, and this is how most scientific journals present them to their readers. (It is also how Figure 1.2 was created and incorporated into this chapter.) But such a non-scalable image is not optimum for new generations of portable mobile e-book readers, which introduce the 'pinch-and-zoom' gesture, allowing instant magnification. A suitably scalable image format, an 'HTML for images', such as SVG (scalable vector graphics) is now more appropriate. Apple has also launched a rich interactive authoring environment (iBooks author)[16] which introduces a much more data-centric metaphor, as compared to the traditional word processor. As such tools mature, we may expect that scientists will be induced to use them in creating journal articles. Whilst in 2013 no journal or book publisher accepts submissions in such a format, we should look out for future developments with interest.

The importance of organizing the content and metadata

In the previous section, I reviewed how scientists and publishers had found the web an easy-to-use interface to search for information in journals, databases and other sources, and discovered how to use it to download documents to their own local computer for further reuse or analysis. As they did so the need for local capabilities to organize this content became increasingly apparent. Here I focus on a type of tool that emerged around 2008 for assisting this process, since it illustrates the increasing (and welcome) adoption of metadata as a content-organizing tool. This problem had in fact been already addressed in quite a different context: the music industry. In the early 2000s, the technology of digitally downloaded music was reinventing a creative industry in many ways not unlike scientific publishing in 2013. Apple Computers introduced iTunes as a new metaphor for a personal music library, and with it the concept of metadata to describe the attributes of the music (artist/author, date released/published, album/publisher, genre/scientific field etc.). One could in general copy a music track from a 'legacy device' (a music CD), drop it into the iTunes library and then go online to acquire further metadata (including, e.g., album art and video). Playlists could be used to define a subset of the music, and copied onto portable listening/viewing devices for the listener's convenience.

Mendeley is an example of a program that adapted this music metaphor to scientific publishing and sharing contexts. Scientific articles, downloaded from a publisher's journal site, can be 'dropped' into the Mendeley article library. This triggers analysis of the metadata attributes of the article, either by pattern scanning to identify bibliographic information such as the authors, the title and so forth (succinctly summarized by the Dublin Core metadata schema)[17] or by inspection of any explicit metadata defined within invisible fields in the document itself. We have ourselves already described how such a harvesting process, using metadata stored directly within an Acrobat file as so-called XMP, can be aggregated and queried in a chemical context.[18] Programs such as Mendeley, which implement much of this concept, offer much more than just a convenient container for a personal library of scientific articles. Such an activated library can be used most simply in conjunction with a word processor as a citation and bibliographic tool when authoring new articles. A more innovative feature of Mendeley is that a selection of articles and the associated metadata can be uploaded to the user's online account and their metadata compared with the 'crowd sourced' content from other Mendeley users. This provides a seamless mechanism for identifying other scientists who may have published on similar topics. One can share such 'playlists' of articles with students and colleagues. Here, however, we see the first signs of the phenomenon of copyright assertion and digital rights management and the associated restrictions that this imposes upon the sharing of research. The implications are expanded upon below. Scientific playlist generation (scientists like to call these their publication lists) can even be automated: Symplectic Elements[19] is a software system that automatically garners all the scientific publications produced by an organization such as a university and organizes them according to the detected metadata. An individual scientist's personal publication record is automatically produced for them, and the system will even generate an h-index[20] as one purported metric of the esteem in which they are held by their colleagues.

The cloud and DRM

I have described above how the online metaphor has evolved between around 1995 and 2010, largely to replace the physical library as the primary mechanism for scientists to have access to shared research. Instead, scientists nowadays build their own personalized digital libraries on physical devices such as desktop computers, organized using metadata to help discoverability. Yet again we might look to the music industry to see how this metaphor might evolve. Most people now have multiple devices on which they can access content, ranging from static desktop computers to smaller portable laptops and to the always-on mobile device. There is no reason why scientists should not access their shared research in a similar manner across this entire device range. A concept known as 'the cloud' has evolved to deliver that content. At its simplest, this removes the user's local computer and storage from the centre of the hub, storing the content, in effect, on a central server-farm. The user purchases or inherits access rights to this content, which can, optionally, be encoded using a mechanism known as digital rights management (DRM).

While the DRM model is currently applied to creative content such as music, video and other forms of entertainment, there are signs that scientific journal articles are also now seen as belonging to the creative industries and subject to the copyright laws that apply to such industries. One such model already operating is known as *Secure Electronic Delivery (SED)*, from the UK British Library. A journal article can be delivered directly to the reader by e-mail as a DRM-enabled PDF attachment. This currently imposes some interesting restrictions.[21]

The recipient:

1   is allowed to make only a single paper copy of the article (it is not clear how enhancements such as Acrobat3D[11] could be invoked on paper), from which they may not make any further paper copies
2   may not convert the file into any other format
3   may not cut and paste or otherwise alter the text
4   may not forward the file to anyone else
5   and after printing the electronic document (once), must then delete it.

The significance of this particular DRM model is that, since the only permitted action upon the received document is to print it (once), it cannot be submitted to a program such as Mendeley to reap the benefits of metadata harvesting. Likewise, it would not be possible to harvest any (digital) data components of the document for electronic reuse (as data). The digital life-cycle or 'ecosystem' in such a model is, in effect, permanently destroyed. This is perhaps an extreme example of how a cloud-based, DRM-protected model may achieve little by way of sharing scientific research. Mechanisms such as this illustrate how critical the delivery mechanism will be to preserving the value of shared information, and how some models may be entirely inappropriate. For example, consider the article[13] in which I discussed how the data associated with that very article might be accessed and reused by readers. If such an article were to be DRM protected, such data components would be likely to be imprisoned by (i.e. to inherit) the DRM applied to the article as a whole, even though the data itself might not be covered by any copyright. Alternatively, one could envisage the different components of an article each having different degrees of DRM, and that this might differ from journal to journal, or between publishers. Would the original authors of an article and its data-based components have any control over how the article was accessed by its readers, via an open access buy-in or other mechanism? It is impossible to predict the answers to these questions, but they demonstrate the challenges ahead, and our need as scientists to keep as much of the world's shared scientific knowledge open as is possible.

The importance of data

The preceding discussion leads us to ask whether journals are still the best medium in which to place data intended for sharing. Data curation has traditionally been largely neglected by scientific journals. When those journals were exclusively printed, the additional (printing) costs of including an appendix or annex with the data frequently precluded its inclusion. Instead, the journal might encourage readers to contact authors directly for such information (assuming they were still contactable). The authors themselves then had to solve the problem of transferring the data into usable form. When electronic dissemination of journals started, authors were asked to include the data in a form that became known as ESI, or electronic supporting information. This was often presented as a single, monolithic PDF file containing a mixture of visual elements, and tables of numbers intermingled with page footers and headers and other non-data. The task of adding semantics to the data fell to the (knowledgeable) reader. Unfortunately, a PDF document is a poor carrier of semantic information and data, and the irrelevant information present in such a document often made copying numbers out of a table an arduous task. That situation largely persists to this day.

Digital repositories

One solution to this problem has emerged in the form of digital data repositories.[22] These differ from the ESI/PDF formats noted above in several key regards:

1   They are OA; no institutional or personal subscription is required.
2   They carry formal and often complete metadata. This includes a date stamp that clearly shows when the data was deposited, with an assurance that it has not been subsequently modified. The metadata itself can be generated automatically from a scripted workflow, ensuring that it is error free and freeing the researcher from the otherwise often onerous task of manual insertion.
3   They carry provenance, in particular the name of the person who deposited the information.
4   They have an associated handle that can be quoted elsewhere, and, as with a DOI, it allows one-click access to the data.
5   The metadata can itself be searched; the data is easily discoverable.
6   The data collection can contain other appropriate identifiers. Thus, data associated with a specific molecule can have a derived and unique identifier known as an InChI key.[23] A digital repository provides an alternative to the scientific journal for scientists to share their data with others, and also a convenient method of claiming priority and ensuring provenance for the data. The handles (DOIs) for this information can themselves be inserted into tables, figures and other components of a traditionally published article. However, the use of a digital repository places the burden of creating this resource upon the scientists themselves, an infrastructure that many may not be willing or able to install.

Recently, however, open services such as Figshare[24] have started to provide an alternative. Among the claimed advantages of such an open repository are the following:

1   All deposited research data is citable (with a DOI).
2   It is cloud based (secure and accessible from anywhere).
3   It is taggable and easily filtered, making the research (data) easily found.
4   Negative results, traditionally difficult to publish in conventional journals, can be archived.
5   Private collaborative spaces to support projects between groups and scientists are available.
6   An API for programmers to interface with their own software is provided.[25]

While the use of digital repositories in this way is not yet common, it is expected to increase in the future.

Social networking mechanisms for sharing research

I have so far focused only on the scientific journal article as the mechanism that most scientists have traditionally used to share their research (another, the scientific conference, should also be noted, even if not here discussed). A highly respected figure in the field of chemistry, Whitesides,[26] urges scientists to explore other mechanisms for making their research shared and accessible, suggesting for example the addition of temporal components such as animations and movies (where appropriate) and that journals routinely support such features (note again the departure from the traditional printable format). It is clear that he also expects the scientific paper to evolve and change even further in the near future. Here I briefly explore the blog (= weblog) as an interesting new addition to the mechanisms for sharing research.

The blog

The first blog appeared in 1999 as an easy procedure for writing a web page. The facility for readers to leave comments is an important part of many blogs. In 2013 this medium is now considered mature and is increasingly being adopted by both individual scientists and publishers as a means of both sharing their research and leaving opinions on that research. The blog can also be a rich carrier of data, and the two can be seamlessly merged into an attractive and enriched environment.[27] Some of the features that make it so include:

- support for citation management[28] and metadata harvesting by means of extensions that, e.g., can resolve a DOI (as defined above) into bibliographic metadata about the article referred to (most journals also include this feature in their production workflow);
- a suitable environment for expressing and rendering mathematical equations within a post;
- support for scalable graphics formats such as SVG (as described above);
- a rich environment for expressing and rendering molecule displays in both two and three dimensions (equivalent to Figure 1.2 above);
- style sheets for customizing the blog for optimal display on mobile devices and tablets;
- functionality that can *chemicalize* a blog. This is a way of identifying chemical terms and molecules contained with a post, and linking these to *pop-ups* that automatically translate, e.g., a chemical name to a chemical structure (Figure 1.1) or to a concept, to further explanation;
- statistics that provide information on post views and search engine terms used to find the post, and which indicate the impact of the blog;
- facility for instant publication;
- permanent archive using services such as WebCite.[29]

The blog provides a mechanism for a single author to share research and ideas. I have used this as a conduit for both my teaching and research activities for some four years now, during which time around 225 posts on diverse topics have appeared. This might be contrasted with my career total of some 330 peer-reviewed articles in scientific journals over a 40-year period. These numbers, of course, imply that the two genres are indeed rather different. A criticism often made of blogs is that they are not peer reviewed, although this can be countered by the observation that posts can attract open comments (peer review is, after all, a closed process) from the community. It is this very feature that improves the science; a commentary on a post can either evince a response from the original poster, or indeed lead to a fully blown conventional article published in a traditional journal. In turn, this article can itself lead to commentaries on other blogs, thus completing the cycle. Seen in this light, the blog post becomes an integral part of the scientific cycle of sharing.

It would, however, be fair to say that most scientists would currently hesitate to use a blog as their primary mechanism for sharing research. Its strengths lie in commentary and discussion of articles found in journals (a form in fact adopted by many publishers who wish to attract a readership) as well as in its being a medium for reporting original research in conjunction with the use of digital repositories. Blogs also have a major pedagogic element, where modern developments are discussed and interpreted for a younger audience of students. Personally, I also find it a suitable medium for sharing whatever experience and knowledge I have acquired over my own career.

The wiki

Like blogs, wikis were initially envisaged as a simple way of creating and sharing a web-based article, albeit with a low learning curve for the authoring process. However, they came to public attention in the form of Wikipedia, a shared compendium of human knowledge with articles authored by more than a million contributors. Once it was adapted to carry rich, reusable chemical information and data[30] (in the manner[31] described above for blogs), we have also found that it is a popular medium for chemistry students to communicate their coursework.[32]

Conclusions

My review covers a period of around 30 years, a small fraction of the time since the first scholarly scientific journals were launched in 1665[33] to share research. During this period we have moved from the institutional or society library as the principal way to deliver printed journals to the research chemist, to a much more complex online environment. Printed journals are by definition not interactive, and the cost of their production limits how much content can be shared on their pages, a limitation that frequently precludes the inclusion of full experimental information and data. In the electronic medium, these and other boundaries are largely removed. I hope that I have given a glimpse of the medium's rich new potential.

Along with this potential come many challenges to be solved. We have barely begun to address the restrictions of, e.g., DRM, and there is a clear need to encourage and educate researchers and teachers to share their science armed with this bewildering array of new tools. Were this review to have been written a mere 15 years into the future, its outcome and format would doubtless have been quite different (you would be unlikely to be reading it as a printed book, for example). Many of the mechanisms outlined above will have been replaced; perhaps even the written word itself will have been largely superseded by the spoken word. But I end as I started, with another apposite quotation from Berra: 'The trouble with our times is that the future is not what it used to be.'[1]

References

1 Berra, Y. (2010) *The Yogi Book*, Workman Publishing. See also www.yogiberra.com/yogi-isms.html.

2 The front page at www.cas.org/content/counter recorded 65,457,839 molecules on 7 March 2012, increased to > 68 million by 4 September 2012.

3 Lewis, G. N. (1916) The Atom and the Molecule, *Journal of the American Chemical Society*, **38**, 762–785. doi: 10.1021/ja02261a002.

4 Rzepa, H. S. (2011) *Computers 1967–2011: a personal perspective. Part 2. 1985–1989*, www.ch.imperial.ac.uk/rzepa/blog/?p=4578. (Archived by WebCite® at www.webcitation.org/65zW2zdhS.)

5 Rzepa, H. S., Murray-Rust, P. and Whitaker, B. J. (1998) The Application of Chemical Multipurpose Internet Mail Extensions (Chemical MIME) Internet Standards to Electronic Mail and World-Wide Web information exchange, *Journal of Chemical Information and Computer Science*, **38**, 976–82. doi: 10.1021/ci9803233.

6 Hull, D., Pettifer, S. R. and Kell, D. B. (2008) Defrosting the Digital Library: bibliographic tools for the next generation web, *PLoS Computational Biology*, **4** e1000204. doi: 10.1371/journal.pcbi.1000204.

7 Rzepa, H. S., Whitaker, B. J. and Winter, M. J. (1994) Chemical Applications of the World-Wide-Web, *Journal of the Chemical Society, Chemical Communications*, 1907.

8 *About the Handle System*, www.handle.net/factsheet.html. (Archived by WebCite® at www.webcitation.org/65zWFosJi.)

9 Paskin, N. (2005) Digital Object Identifiers for Scientific Data, *Data Science Journal*, **4**, 12–20. doi: 10.2481/dsj.4.12.

10 CrossRef.org, www.doi.org/factsheets/DOIKeyFacts.html.

11 Kumar, I. P., Ziegler, A., Ziegler, J., Uchanska-Ziegler, B. and Zeigler, A. (2008) Grasping Molecular Structures through Publication-integrated 3D Models, *Trends in Biochemical Science*, **33**, 408–12.

12 Murray-Rust, P. and Rzepa, H. S. (1999) Chemical Markup Language and XML: Part I. Basic principles, *Journal of Chemical Information and Computer Science*, **39**, 928. doi: 10.1021/ci990052b.

13 Rzepa, H. S. (2011) The Past, Present and Future of Scientific Discourse, *Chemoinformatics*, **3**, 36. doi: 10.1186/1758-2946-3-46.

14 Webb, J. *What to Expect in EPUB3*, http://radar.oreilly.com/2011/01/epub3-preview.html. (Archived by WebCite® at www.webcitation.org/5wo1jdC3L on 27-02-2011.)

15 Lawson, B. and Sharp, R. *Introducing HTML5*, http://introducinghtml5.com/. (Archived by WebCite® at www.webcitation.org/5wo1yKHbs on 27-02-2011.) See also http://dev.w3.org/html5/spec/Overview.html. (Archived by WebCite® at www.webcitation.org/5wo1o6RPx on 27-02-2011.)

16 *Apple Computer*, iBooks Author, www.apple.com/ibooks-author/. (Archived by WebCite® at www.webcitation.org/65zWoElsn.)

17 Dublin Core Metadata Initiative, http://dublincore.org/.

18 Casher, O. and Rzepa, H. S. (2006) SemanticEye: a Semantic Web application to rationalise and enhance chemical electronic publishing, *Journal of Chemical Information Models*, **46**, 2396–411. doi: 10.1021/ci060139e.

19 Symplectic, www.symplectic.co.uk/.

20 Hirsch, J. (2005) An Index to Quantify an Individual's Scientific Research Output, *Proceedings of the National Academy of Sciences*, **102**, 16569–16572. doi: 10.1073/pnas.0507655102.

21 British Library Document Supply Service, www.bl.uk/reshelp/atyourdesk/docsupply/help/receiving/deliveryoptions/electronic/sed/sedfaq/index.html. (Archived by WebCite® at

www.webcitation.org/65zX6HyeC).

22 Downing, J., Murray-Rust, P., Tonge, A. P., Morgan, P., Rzepa, H. S., Cotterill, F., Day, N. and Harvey, M. J. (2008) SPECTRa: the deposition and validation of primary chemistry research data in digital repositories, *Journal of Chemical Information Models*, **48**, 1571–1581. doi: 10.1021/ci7004737.

23 See www.iupac.org/home/publications/e-resources/inchi.html.

24 Hahnell, M., http://figshare.com/.

25 Rzepa, H. S., *Digital Repositories. An update*, www.ch.imperial.ac.uk/rzepa/blog/?p=7290 (Archived by WebCite® at www.webcitation.org/6AQKiyn3w). An example of such an automated deposition can be found at doi: 10.6084/m9.figshare.93114.

26 Whitesides, G., www.youtube.com/embed/NHuC5yZeHYQ.

27 Rzepa, H. S. *The Blog Post as a Scientific Article: citation management*, www.ch.imperial.ac.uk/rzepa/blog/?p=6341. (Archived by WebCite® at www.webcitation.org/65zXdiHXL.)

28 See, for example, http://knowledgeblog.org/kcite-plugin, and http://knowledgeblog.org/kblog-metadata.

29 Webcite, www.webcitation.org/.

30 Walker, M. A. (2010) Wikipedia as a Resource for Chemistry. In Belford, R., Moore, J. and Pence, H. (eds) *Enhancing Learning with Online Resources, Social Networking, and Digital Libraries*. ACS Symposium Series, **1060**, 79–92. doi:10.1021/bk-2010-1060.ch005.

31 Rzepa, H. S. *Jmol and WordPress: loading 3D molecular models, molecular isosurfaces and molecular*, www.ch.imperial.ac.uk/rzepa/blog/?p=8. (Archived by WebCite® at www.webcitation.org/660NLRmSP.)

32 Rzepa, H. S., Bearpark, M. J., Armstrong, A. and Hunt, P. Activating Computational Chemistry via an Online Presence, *Abstracts of Papers, 237th ACS National Meeting, Salt Lake City, UT, United States, 22–26 March*.

33 Hooke, R. (1665) An Accompt of the Improvement of Optick Glasses, *Philosophical Transactions*, **1**, 2–3. doi: 10.1098/rstl.1665.0003.

2

Supporting qualitative research in the humanities and social sciences: using the Mass Observation Archive

Fiona Courage and Jane Harvell

ABSTRACT

This chapter uses the Mass Observation Archive (MOA), a vast collection of qualitative data on many subject themes, as a case study to examine how the availability of new technologies and tools for research has changed the way in which information professionals can support the use of data of this nature in the humanities and social sciences. It explores the different ways in which research in these disciplines can be supported through digitization, and outlines how important it is to ensure that there is a 'curatorial voice' for the researcher in digital material, showing how this adds value to the resource. The chapter also details the various projects with which Mass Observation has been involved to open up and enhance the usability of the Archive. These include the JISC-funded Observing the 1980s Open Educational Resource project, which offers opportunities for the reuse of newly digitized material under a Creative Commons licence, and the SALDA project which produced sets of openly available Linked Data extracted from the records of the MOA Catalogue. By working closely with academics and information professionals on projects such as these, the authors of this chapter argue, they have been able to offer many new ways for researchers in the social sciences and the humanities and other disciplines to use and manipulate the collection.

Introduction

The availability of new technologies and tools for research in humanities and social sciences has changed the ways in which information professionals can support the use of qualitative data in humanities and social sciences. Recent years have seen a large increase in the number of digitization and metadata creation projects undertaken by libraries and archives across the world, underpinned by a firm acknowledgement from the research community that these resources are required in order to enhance and support work in various subject areas. Researchers are encouraged to use technologies to create cross-disciplinary and cross-institutional collaborations in their work; and by easing accessibility to qualitative data resources, we can support these initiatives, as well as encourage the use of our unique and valuable resources.

For many years the Mass Observation Archive (MOA, www. massobs.org.uk/index.htm), based at the University of Sussex, has provided researchers with a vast collection of qualitative data on many subject themes. Over the last ten years, the Archive has been involved in various digitization and metadata projects that use technology to increase the accessibility of the collection. We shall look at the use of the MOA, offering a case study that examines both the common and the different elements of user support required by social sciences and humanities disciplines and how these might also be used to initiate and support collaborative research.

Mass Observation

Mass Observation was established in 1937 as a social observation project in which people around the country were recruited to become what Mass Observation's founders described as 'the cameras with which we are trying to photograph contemporary life',[1] constructing an organization that used a combination of ethnographic survey and reflective personal writing project to record everyday life in Britain. Between 1937 and the mid-1950s, over 2000 members of the public contributed to the National Panel of volunteer writers, sending in diary accounts of their daily lives and responding to monthly open-ended questionnaires designed to elicit personal and subjective accounts of opinion and experience in contemporary Britain.

The purpose of all this activity was to give the opportunity for ordinary people to make their views heard, and to provide access to these views to researchers from all fields. Initially, various publications, journal articles, newspaper reports and broadcasts resulted from some of the findings, but ultimately much of the collected data was never used. The archive of material amassed in this initial project was eventually brought to the University of Sussex to be opened as a public access archive, thereby fulfilling the original intention of making the information available to all who might want to use it.

The Mass Observation Project

The availability of the original project material inspired the establishment of a second phase of data collection, beginning in 1981 under the direction of Professor David Pocock and Dorothy Sheridan. The concept of a National Panel of Volunteer Writers was reawakened, and a new batch of volunteers recruited to respond to questionnaires reflecting on and recording late 20th-century life. The Project[2] has continued unbroken since 1981, issuing three questionnaires or 'Directives' a year, normally dealing with three different themes. Currently over 300 themes have been covered, spanning topics as diverse as from general elections to gardening, reactions to 9/11, and hair and hairdressing. The themes are often prompted by world events and current affairs, but over 30% have been commissioned by researchers who have opted to use the Mass Observation as one of their data sources.

The panel size averages around 500 members, some responding to only one or two Directives, while others have contributed for over 30 years. This provides a huge potential for longitudinal qualitative research: a data set of case studies reaching back years, if not decades, for researchers to access. Responses vary from one or two pages of writing to many pages of narrative, which may include photographs or ephemera. The unifying factor for these diverse responses is the qualitative nature of the material.

The Project often attracts criticism that the panel is not representative of modern-day Britain, and indeed over the years there has been a slide towards a preponderance of older women keen to contribute. Various attempts have been made to redress this since 1981, including the introduction of acceptance criteria in 2004, in the Project's first significant attempt to recruit writers from areas of the population previously under-represented. Mass Observation does not seek to establish social classification or ethnic background for its contributors, but it is likely that ethnic minorities are under-represented, and there seems to be a higher representation of urban dwellers.

The former Director of the MOA, Professor Dorothy Sheridan, believes that much of the discomfort about using self-selected groups such as the Mass Observation panel stems from 'a common belief about what constitutes *proper* or scientific social research'.[3] Professor Sheridan illustrates how researchers from different disciplines encounter this type of data, in particular historians, for whom:

> such material is a delight and a challenge because it may be all we have left of a particular life and time: a crucial part of the scholarly task is to establish the relationship between what has survived and its historical moment, that is, how 'representative' can we take it to be and of what.[3]

Unlike many other data sets designed and produced for specific projects, the data collected by the Mass Observation Project is available for any researcher to use as soon as it becomes available. Even in instances where a researcher has commissioned a theme, he does not have exclusive access to the material collected. So there are opportunities for different disciplinary interpretations of a single set of data. While this offers the possibility of exciting synergies and new opportunities, at the same time it places more importance on our role as data collectors, data controllers, interpreters and ethical advisers in our support for researchers.

Researcher use of Mass Observation

The MOA receives around 800 visits per year, mainly from students and academics, the majority of whom have humanities backgrounds. The purpose of most of these visits, made mostly by humanities scholars, particularly historians, is to look at the material collected largely between 1937 and the 1950s. Similarly, those looking at the post-1981 Mass Observation Project are largely from humanities-based disciplines, with history researchers again predominating. This is in direct contrast to the profile of the researchers who commission new Directives from Mass Observation and are therefore seeking 'contemporary' data. In those Directives commissioned since 1991, 11 disciplines are represented: 78% have been commissioned by social science researchers, 16% by humanities and 6% sciences. These two distinct types of usage illustrate how a single resource can be used in different ways by different disciplines: humanities scholars tend to use the collection as a historical archive or primary source evidence, while social scientists use it as a way of assembling a contemporary data set.

Supporting research use through digitization

Perhaps the greatest change in the way user support has been delivered to researchers in recent years is the rise in the availability of online resources, including digital facsimiles of archival materials. Over a decade ago the benefits of using digitized materials were becoming more apparent, providing easy availability at a location and time convenient to the researcher, and the ability to perform searches and make copies of material more easily than when using microforms or originals.[4] Advances in technology have served to make these factors even more useful to the researcher, with improvements in tools such as Optical Character Recognition (OCR) providing enhanced searchability and legibility for many resources. Despite these advances, it is acknowledged that many humanities scholars, and to a lesser extent social scientists, are less advanced than scientists in their adoption of digital resources as primary tools for working with archival collections.[5] This highlights the need for analytical tools and services to become more sophisticated and transparent for the humanities community to use; these scholars are, for example, often in search of nice physical distinctions that are sometimes lost in the transition to digital format, and rely heavily on metadata to identify and compare variants. The creation of this metadata naturally falls to the librarian and archivist, whose cataloguing and curatorial skills enable them to develop transparent and easy-to-use digital resources to act as strong surrogates for original hard-copy primary sources.

The MOA illustrates how a primary-source resource used chiefly by humanities researchers has been digitized, and equipped with tools and data designed in conjunction with archive staff to support researchers. In 2006 the MOA embarked on a partnership with the commercial publishing company Adam Matthew Digital (www.amdigital.co.uk) to create a digital resource, Mass Observation Online.[6] Throughout this project sequential tranches of the Archive from 1937 to the 1950s have been digitized and released for sale around the world, with over 80% of purchasers being outside the UK. By 2015 the entire holdings of this first phase Mass Observation (1937–1950s) will have been published in this way.

The publisher's statistics indicate that Mass Observation Online (MO Online) has received increasingly heavy use since publication, with over 19,500 unique visits by users from institutions that have purchased the resource worldwide between 2008 and 2011. Despite the extent of material already available electronically, the statistics for actual visits by UK and international researchers to access the Archive at the University of Sussex have remained stable. This would seem to indicate that, far from undermining the use of the physical Archive, digitization has widened accessibility and thus increased usage.

Digitizing the collection has also brought a level of flexibility in the way that researchers use the Archive that is not offered by the physical collection. As noted in the Research Information Network's (RIN) Report (2007), scholars engage with a range of resources and technologies, mixing digital with hard copy, and are prepared to adopt new technologies in order to improve their current practices:

> They have become used to managing digital resources and this has freed them to access and use information which is in locations far from its source. Moreover, the very nature of digital technologies has enabled researchers to create and assemble information in new ways in the course of their research, presenting new issues to them ...[7]

Publishers and creators of these digital resources must understand that these demands determine the value of digitizing primary source material. As part of the creation of MO Online, specific tools have been developed in response to researchers' expressed needs. One example is a mapping tool that allows researchers to identify diarists in the same region of the UK quickly and easily, without needing to interrogate a database.

For humanities researchers the ability to follow themes and individuals through the collection is important. The large, hard-copy collection of diaries have no subject index and are held in chronological order, so that a researcher looking for a specific subject needs to trawl through them in search of relevant material. Equally, if researchers want to track an individual diarist, they need to go through a box of material for each month that the diarist wrote. Digitization has provided the opportunity for researchers to create their own indexes, while, with a few clicks of a mouse, they are now able to pull up a listing of individual diarists and then trawl through all that they have written, rather than having to plough through the diary entries of hundreds of other diarists. In some cases OCR technology has been used to create searchable rich text.

However, it is worth noting that one of the key findings of RIN's report *Reinventing Research?*[8] was that although

> they are reluctant on occasion to consult texts that require a trip to a distant library or archive[; n]evertheless, none of the participants is yet ready to abandon print and manuscript resources in favour of digital ones. Rather, they engage with a range of resources and technologies, moving seamlessly between them.

This report concluded that 'Such behaviours are likely to persist for some time'.[8]

The curatorial voice in a digital world

The use of digital proxies has strong implications for user support. Unlike for personal visitors to the Archive, there is no member of staff on hand to explain the intricacies of catalogues or the context of collection holdings. So it is important to ensure that the digital resource replicates the 'curatorial voice' for the researcher. The need for an effective 'curatorial voice' highlights the importance of collaboration between curator and publisher to develop a coherent set of guidelines, not only to help researchers to understand the resource, but also to offer them as profound a user experience as they might have in person. Working closely with Mass Observation, Adam Matthew Digital was very careful to provide this voice and context, so adding value for researchers in their use of MO Online:

> When creating our digital resources, we always strive to create a sense of context, which is absolutely essential if users are to research effectively online. Without this, users may find themselves unable to understand or navigate the archival content. This sense of context can be created by careful consideration of how to organize the digital material (in MO Online's case, we tried to be as

consistent as possible with the physical arrangement of the archives); but also through use of secondary resources aimed at different user levels, such as essays designed for undergraduates or for researchers, which can recreate the invaluable experience of being shown round an archive by a 'real' curator. Even the front end design of the website can help build an 'atmosphere' that suggests ways to approach the source material. By these means we hope that users can be guided to understanding what the digital archives offers them.

(Martha Fogg, Senior Development Director, Adam Matthew Digital)

The sympathetically re-created 'curatorial voice' available on MO Online means that the electronic resource goes beyond the mere provision of a corpus of digitized material, and also provides context for users of this large and unusual collection.

All these features have ensured that the digitized resource can become an invaluable part of the ways in which the collection is used, both remotely and *in situ*, thereby adding value to the material object.

Mass Observation as data set collection/collector

As stated earlier, humanities scholars tend to use the collection as a historical archive or as primary source material, while social scientists use it as a means of collecting a contemporary data set. Social scientists, in particular sociologists, dominate the numbers of researchers using Directives as a data set for their research and have commissioned 78% of Directives issued since 1991. The questionnaire is currently drafted by Mass Observation staff in collaboration with the commissioning academic, and sent to the Panel as part of a regular mailing. Responses are collated by Archive staff and made available in the reading rooms to any researcher within three months of the mailing date. This material has not yet been digitized and made publicly available.

An interesting pattern of usage has evolved among the social scientists who commission these Directives. Unlike many of the humanities scholars, who visit the reading rooms in person and work through boxes of hard-copy material from various themes, social scientists often request copies of the entire set of responses to a single Directive theme. These responses are sometimes used as case studies for qualitative analysis, and offer the potential for longitudinal study of individuals in order to track changes in habit and opinion by looking at individuals' responses to similar themes over a period of time.[9] Coding the responses is also a common practice among social scientists, sometimes using specialized software such as Atlas (www.atlasti.com) (qualitative data analysis and research software), sometimes by simply cutting and pasting data into tables and applying specific word searches to identify and analyse patterns.

While new Directives are often used as data sets, within a short space of time they can also be used as primary source material for other disciplines. As information professionals, it is our duty to make the information available in a way that will best serve the different needs of social science and humanities researchers, alongside researchers from other disciplines who may use the material. So it is important for the material to be catalogued and described in ways that transcend such distinctions and enhance the potential for future discovery and collaboration.

Tools for support

Creating high-quality metadata and data documentation can help the user interpret raw data sources.[10]

The information professional's role is to provide support for users of information resources: at its most basic, this means letting the user know what information is available. Metadata ensures the accessibility of a collection, by allowing users to interrogate and manipulate data as they need. While the International Standard for Archival Description (ISAD[G]) (www.icacds.org.uk/eng/standards.htm) has been used to catalogue the MOA and make it accessible to users through the CALM (www.axiell.co.uk/calm) archival management system, we have also consistently sought to augment this information with supplementary metadata to make it more searchable. As Louise Corti, Associate Director at the UK Data Archive (www.data-archive.ac.uk) notes:

Users of qualitative data want easy access to data and they want more than just raw data. *Enhancing* collections so they can be used more easily and effectively should be central to an archive's mission. It is never just about preserving original research documents.[11]

In 2009–10 a retrospective cataloguing project listed each individual response to Mass Observation Directives since 1981 into the CALM database. Prior to this, a researcher would not have known the number of responses to a specific Directive. The project has created a metadata record for every response to each Directive, thus providing researchers with details of each item and its writer. This means that a list of all the responses submitted from each individual writer can now be generated, a process that previously could be accomplished only by archive staff using card catalogues, which was both lengthy and costly. Researchers are now able to identify individual resources they would like to access, follow up lines of enquiry, and pinpoint potential case studies for their work.

In 2010 another project designed to enhance the accessibility of information about the MOA was undertaken. Funded under the JISC Infrastructure for Resources Discovery Programme,[12] the Sussex Archive Linked Data Application (SALDA) project[13] extracted metadata from 23,000 MOA catalogue records in the CALM system. This data was converted into Linked Data (http://linkeddata.org) and made publicly available using an Open Licence via Talis Platform (www.talis.com/ platform). In addition to creating a set of Linked Data, the project allowed the Archive staff to become familiar with ways of transforming data in this way, and created new possibilities for the creation of wider resource-discovery networks.

Sharing data and making it available through other portals and institutions is a valuable way of raising the visibility of collections and making them useful to researchers.

A current JISC-funded project, Observing the 1980s,[14] is being undertaken to create Open Educational Resources (OERs), using material collected as part of the Mass Observation Project in the 1980s and sound recordings held in the British Library. These OERs are primarily designed for learning and teaching, but an off-shoot of this project is the creation of standardized summaries of items, by means of which they can be identified and classified. These summaries, or enhanced metadata, will be deposited at Qualidata (www.esds.ac.uk) and thus become openly available to an even wider range of researchers.

Changing research needs – collaboration

A key change in humanities research over the past 10–15 years has been the growth of formal and systematic collaboration between researchers. This is a response in part to new funding opportunities, but also to the possibilities opened up by new technology.[8]

Researchers are working with new technologies to use resources collaboratively in increasingly diverse ways. Information professionals can support research by providing environments conducive to interaction between scholars, encouraging them to develop synergies relating to specific resources.

In 2006 Mass Observation set up a JISCMail (www.jiscmail.ac.uk/) list to encourage researchers and those interested in Mass Observation to join discussions regarding the collection and to share experiences of using the material in their research. The establishment of this list reflected Mass Observation's original objective of mass collaboration with the aim of gathering information and making it available to all who might usefully use it.

Other collaborative research projects include the University of Brighton-funded collaborative research network Methodological Innovations: Using Mass Observation,[15] a vibrant collective of researchers within the University from arts, humanities and social science backgrounds working together to create opportunities to share research works and establish new areas of collaborative research.

It's about people as well as resources and technology!

By organizing and participating in conferences, seminar series and events we can highlight the potential for using collections as a research resource, as well as illustrate the range of support that we can give. Taking advantage of its 75th anniversary year, Mass Observation has organized a public lecture series and an academic conference, drawing on speakers who have used the collection in a variety of ways.[16] Each event provides the opportunity for researchers to network and find out how others have used the Archive. These occasions, which bring scholars, the general public and Mass Observers themselves together are building on experience gained from previous successful events, such as the conference organized by Mass

Observation in 2007. They provide opportunities for researchers to publicize their research and interests within a 'market-place' of posters and displays. Events such as these create tremendous possibilities for networking and identifying potential partners for future collaboration.

Curating ethics

Finally, Mass Observation acts as collector, guardian and gatekeeper of data collected under its aegis. Responses are anonymized before being provided to researchers, and any interaction with the panel is handled by Mass Observation staff. As curators, we are bound to protect the subjects of the material as carefully as we protect the material itself.

In a paper on the challenges of web access to archival oral history in Britain, the Oral History Curator at the British Library, Dr Rob Perks, discusses how keepers of materials exercise control over access. He argues that changing the way in which researchers access data (in this case via the internet) transforms the guardianship relationship that we, as curators, have with our material. He claims that this can make us feel uncomfortable, as 'we fear a marginalization of our own role as conduit, explainer and interpreter'.[17]

Throughout this process it is vital that, as curators, we communicate the reasons for our actions to researchers so as to develop a culture of trust for both the organization and the data it collects. We are able to support researchers in developing research ethics suited to their particular discipline's use of qualitative data both generally and, more specifically, when it is garnered from Mass Observation.

Conclusion

Success for the Archive comes with strong academic involvement in creating new data sets and providing access to the collection as a single archive. Responsible storage and accessibility of good-quality metadata are vital to ensure that the Mass Observation materials are easily discoverable and open. By working closely with academics and information profession colleagues we have been able to create projects and tools to enable researchers from the social sciences, humanities and other disciplines to use and manipulate this vast collection of unique qualitative data. It is important that we present an archive that researchers can trust as an established resource with a long-standing academic reputation. This chimes nicely with the assertion in the RIN report:

it seems more likely that concerns over the vulnerability of socially-created valuable information will send researchers into the arms of those they trust – on curation and preservation issues at the very least.[7]

References

1 Harrisson, T. H. and Madge, C. (1938) *First Year's Work 1937–1938*, Lindsay Drummond.

2 www.massobs.org.uk/mass_observation_project.html.

3 Sheridan, D. (1996) *'Damned Anecdotes and Dangerous Confabulations': Mass Observation as life history*, Mass Observation Occasional Paper Series No. 7, University of Sussex Library.

4 Duff, W. M. and Cherry, J. M. (2000) Use of Historical Documents in a Digital World: comparisons with original materials and microfiche, *Information Research*, **6** (1).

5 Borgman, C. (2009) The Digital Future Is Now: a call to action for the humanities, *Digital Humanities Quarterly*, **3** (4).

6 www.amdigital.co.uk/Collections/Mass-Observation-Online.aspx.

7 Research Information Network (2007) *Researchers' Use of Academic Libraries and Their Services*, London.

8 Research Information Network (2011) *Reinventing Research? Information practices in the humanities*, London.

9 Busby, H. (2000) *Health, Sickness and the Work Ethic*, Mass Observation Occasional Paper Series No. 11, University of Sussex Library.

10 Corti, L. (2005) User Support, *Forum: Qualitative Social Research*, **6** (2), Art. 41.

11 Corti, L. (2011) The European Landscape of Qualitative Social Research Archives: methodological and practical issues, *Forum: Qualitative Social Research*, **12** (3), Art. 11.

12 www.jisc.ac.uk/whatwedo/programmes/inf11/infrastructureforresourcediscovery.aspx.

13 http://blogs.sussex.ac.uk/salda/about.

14 http://blogs.sussex.ac.uk/observingthe80s/about.

15 www.brighton.ac.uk/sass/research/massobservation.

16 www.massobs.org.uk/conference.htm.

17 Perks, R. (2009) The Challenges of Web Access to Archival Oral History in Britain, *IASA Journal*, **32**.

3

Researchers and scholarly communications: an evolving interdependency

David C. Prosser

ABSTRACT

Scholarly communication is not just about communication. It is not the final stage of the publication process, solely a means of providing the 'minutes of science'. Rather, it is a vital part of the research process itself, inspiring researchers along new avenues of discovery and enabling the creation of connections between concepts and people. The ways in which researchers disseminate their research have changed and developed over the four centuries since the launch of the first scientific journals. But it can be argued that scholarly communication has in turn affected the way in which researchers behave. This chapter explores some of the interaction and interdependencies between researchers and scholarly communication. It also describes how the move to online, electronic publishing might further influence the research process.

Introduction

We tend to think of the history of scholarly journal publishing as an unbroken thread of consistent activity since the founding of the first journals. In reality, journals have changed in many ways over the past 350 odd years, and so has the research environment. It may be obvious that publishing activity will alter in order to reflect changes in the research process, but it may also be argued that the research process itself has changed, at least in part, as a result of developments in scholarly communication. This chapter will investigate the two-way flow of influence between research and publishing, in terms both of a 400-year history and of looking forward to new developments.

The rise of journals

The birth of the modern system of scholarly communications is generally taken to be the launching of the first two scientific journals, the *Journal des Sçavans* in 1665 and the *Philosophical Transactions of the Royal Society* in 1666. These journals reflected the growing interest in natural philosophy at the time, but also, through their very existence, began to initiate changes in scholarly practice. Before the mid-seventeenth century it was not the norm for 'scientists' (to use an anachronism: they would not have recognized the term) to share their findings. While they were as concerned with issues of priority as are modern researchers – witness the famously bitter battle between Newton and Liebnitz regarding the invention of calculus – they were hoarders of knowledge, reluctant to give what we would describe as a competitive advantage to their rivals. This led to some wondrous contortions, not the least of which was Galileo's 'announcement' of his discovery of the rings of Saturn in 1610. Galileo wanted to be able to prove priority, but did not want actually to release the information, so his announcement took the form of a 37-letter anagram in Latin, which even if solved would prove to be unhelpfully cryptic.

It was within this environment of secrecy that Henry Oldenburg, the first publisher of the *Philosophical Transactions*, had to operate. To overcome the natural reluctance of researchers, Oldenburg wrote to all the leading scientists of the day stressing the advantages of publication as a means of establishing priority. If the discovery was described in black and white there could be no quibbles over who the discoverer was. So from the very start a major incentive for publication was not communication to one's peers in the hope that they may be able to build upon the work described, but rather a desire to prove one's priority and intellectual worth.

As time passed, research (particularly in the sciences) became industrialized and professionalized. By the mid-nineteenth century 'amateur' scholars such as Darwin, who lived as a country gentleman with inherited wealth, worked in parallel with a growing number of professionals, such as Faraday, who was employed by the Royal Institution. Darwin was notoriously reluctant to publish his findings and theories. He was compelled to publish his first paper on natural selection only because he wanted to establish his priority over (or at least independence from) Wallace, who was about to publish a remarkably similar theory. Darwin's general reluctance to publish is often attributed to both his perfectionist nature and his concern over the reaction to the perceived blasphemous nature of his theories. But perhaps it was also that Darwin did not need to publish. He was seeking no grants, nor did he have employers to appease or Research Excellence Framework returns to consider. As an independent researcher he was free from the compulsion of 'publish or perish'.

Faraday, on the other hand, published regularly, and had over 45 papers under his name in the *Philosophical Transactions*. True, he was more of an experimentalist than was Darwin, but the key difference was that Faraday was an employee, a professional scientist, whose publication record formed evidence of his skill as a researcher. Although he was not formally judged on the number of papers he published, it is clear that publication was a means of establishing both priority and prestige for Faraday (and, by extension, the Royal Institution).

So, in less than 200 years we can witness a shift from researchers as secretive hoarders of knowledge to researchers as published self-publicists.

The role of journals

As we have seen, communication is not necessarily the only, or even the most important, part of scholarly communication. In fact, journal publishing has traditionally been described as fulfilling four functions: registration, certification, awareness, and archiving.[1] That is:

- Registration: The author wishes to ensure that s/he is acknowledged as the person who carried out a specific piece of research and made a specific discovery.
- Certification: Through the process of independent peer review it is determined that the author's claims are reasonable.
- Awareness: The research is communicated to the author's peer group.
- Archiving: The research is retained for posterity.

Obviously, the weight assigned by researchers to each of these functions will vary, depending on their role as either author or reader. Registration, as described above, is most important for authors, as it is the means by which they can stake a claim to the research. Certification benefits both authors and readers. For authors it improves the quality of their work (by providing independent feedback) and allows it to enter the scientific record as a valid piece of research. For the readers, certification guarantees to what they read a certain level of quality and relevance.

Awareness ensures that the author's work is widely known (increasing the chance that their work will be read and cited) and ensures that readers will be able to find the works that they need. The guarantee of long-term archiving gives authors comfort that they will forever be associated with a particular piece of work and readers the reassurance that they will be able to find historical research in the scientific record.

An emergent function of the scholarly communication system is that it provides input into the scholarly reward structure. There is increasing competition for academic posts and for research grants (for example, the UK's Medical Research Council currently funds only 15% of grant requests). Administrators (both within institutions and in funding agencies) need means by which they can rank researchers and separate the funded from the unfunded. Increasingly they have turned to researchers' publication histories for this, working on the basis that past results are an indicator of future success. Ideally, the quality of individual papers should be assessed. But this is a huge task, and administrators look to the standing of the journal to act as a proxy for the quality of the research and the researcher.

The most famous proxy of quality is the Impact Factor, published by Thomson Reuters. The Impact Factor (IF) is a measure of the average number of citations that papers published in the journal in a given year received in a defined time-window. The problems with using the IF as a proxy for the quality of individual papers are well documented (and have been highlighted even by their creator, Eugene Garfield).[2] Not least is the fact that in even the most highly cited journals a significant proportion of papers receive no citations. At best, the IF tells you that your work is in good company, not that it necessarily has merit in itself. But for many the convenience of the IF and its reassuringly scientific-looking accuracy to three decimal places outweigh the problems, and some funders have gone so far as to reward preferentially researchers who have managed to get their papers published in high-impact journals, irrespective of the intrinsic quality of the research. Fundamentally, researchers do not just want to publish good research, they want to publish in the highest-impact journals that they can, or at the least in a journal covered by Thomson Reuters. There is a perceived hierarchy of journals in each field (based mainly on IF rating), and authors want to publish as far up this hierarchy as possible. The greater the kudos of the journal, the greater the kudos of the researcher, and the greater the chance of a future promotion or research grant.

This use of journal quality to make funding and promotion decisions is a clear example of how the scholarly communications system has had a direct effect on the way in which research is done.

Electronic futures

It is remarkable that despite the ubiquity of the internet over the past 20 years it has had little impact on the fundamentals underpinning journal publishing. This may appear surprising – what about online access, citation links between papers, Big Deals, etc.? Certainly, the delivery mechanism has obviously changed beyond recognition. No longer is a publisher required to package papers into bundles to form print issues, to be posted around the world (taking weeks or months to reach the customer) and placed on library shelves to be perused by researchers (or, more likely, graduate students on their behalf). Today, access is 24/7, at the desktop – for those affiliated with a subscribing institution. And new business models such as Big Deals (where libraries purchase electronic access to a publisher's entire output rather than to selected titles) mean access to more content – again for those affiliated with a subscribing institution. New thinking around business models has also led to the Open Access (OA) movement and this will, I believe, soon become the dominant business model for scholarly journals in the internet age.

But while electronic journals, Big Deals and OA are important in themselves, they are 'only' variations on the existing access mechanisms and business models. They have had almost no impact on the content of journals. It is true that citations can now link straight through to papers, protein names can be linked to databases, and suchlike, but the underlying nature of journal articles is the same today as it was 50 years ago. They retain their decades-old structure and are still written in a rather stilted, international style that many claim is not conducive either to communication or to the reproducibility of results.

To look at what scholarly communication can be, we need to separate the functions of a journal as described above. We need to accept that a document that allows for a means of conferring reputation on a researcher may not be the same as a document that transmits the maximum amount of information.

One factor that will affect how papers are written is the changing way in which papers are read. There have been complaints of information overload since the beginning of written communications, so we must take today's complaints with a small pinch of salt. But one thing is indisputable: the literature is growing, and the extent of discipline range in which any given researcher can hope to retain mastery is ever narrowing. As an example, a search of PubMed for papers published in 2011 with 'HIV' in the title returns 8500 hits – a publication rate of approximately one paper an hour over the course of the year. If we extend the search to both title and abstract we get over 13,500 hits; and a search in the same period for 'HIV' or 'AIDS' gives almost 17,000 returns – one article published almost every 30 minutes. In many fields the literature is growing more quickly than practitioners can hope to read it. And this assumes that researchers will read only in their own field. A scientist who wishes to gain insights from similar research in other fields will have an even greater mass of literature to read.

Data mining

Thankfully, technology gives us one way of tackling the ever-growing volume of literature. The emerging fields of text and data mining use computers to scour the literature, looking for connections between papers that human readers may not have made. A researcher studying the causes of epilepsy may not realize that their work has implications for those studying the causes of migraines (and vice versa). These researchers would have no cause to read the literature in the others' field. But text mining could discover the links, to the potential benefit of both fields.

There are a number of barriers to the successful uptake of text and data mining. Not least is the fact that most publishers do not automatically allow text mining of their corpus even if the researcher's institution is paying for access. The researcher needs to contact the publisher and ask for permission. An example of the problems this causes was highlighted by the Wellcome Trust as part of a case study on data mining in the field of malaria. The Trust began by compiling a corpus of potentially interesting papers related to the study of malaria. What it discovered was that these papers represented output from almost 100 different publishers. Somebody wishing to data mine the papers would need to gain permission from each of the publishers – a massive administrative burden.[3]

In the UK, the Hargreaves *Review of Intellectual Property and Growth* (2011) has recommended that a copyright exception be introduced to allow text and data mining of content to which customers have legal access (for example through subscriptions).[4] This has been fiercely contested by publishers, presumably as they view text and data mining services as a future revenue-generating opportunity. Nonetheless the recommendation has recently been accepted by the government.

But practical considerations aside, a bigger question relates to the nature of information. If the predictions that papers will increasingly be read by machines rather than by humans proves to be true, then surely these papers should be written in a style that makes them easier for machines to read? Why surround them with the trappings that humans need in order to render them readable? Publication could then be the expression of facts in a machine-readable way. The facts would not necessarily have to possess the 'novelty' or import that is traditionally expected of a paper-worthy result; and negative results could be included more easily than they are at present. (There is a perceived bias against publishing null and negative results, even though they can provide interesting and useful data points.) This would give a much richer database of information out of which new connections could be discovered.

Of course, for this to work, new reward and citation structures would be required. An emergent discovery that comes about from the data mining of 10,000 genetics papers cannot possibly cite all the papers and credit all the authors. The power of this method will come from the aggregation of massive data sets, not necessarily from individual genius and insight. And if we move away from citation, then we potentially move away from the IF which currently serves as an easy means of assessment for administrators.

In fact, it could be argued that the reason why scholarly communication in the internet age looks so similar to scholarly communication in the print age is precisely because the needs of promotion, tenure and granting committees outweigh the needs of communication and instil a certain inertia into the system which prevents a move to new systems of greater utility. There are a few ways in which this inertia could be overcome. One would be for far-sighted funders to revise completely the ways in which they assess researchers and their worth.

Another way in which a change in the system might happen would be if we found that we could no longer afford the current means of scholarly communication. The serials crisis is well known, and although the move to online and Big Deals (which gave access to increased numbers of titles for much the same cost) provided temporary respite we now see a number of libraries having to cancel titles. But there are also less well-known hidden costs, such as those associated with peer review. It has been estimated that peer review costs the UK approximately £200 million per year in reviewers' time.[5] Many journal editors complain that it is becoming increasingly difficult to find reviewers (although this may be a perennial complaint of journal editors). For their part, reviewers complain that they are asked to review papers for one journal that they have already rejected for another. It may prove to be that the entire peer-review, subscription journal model becomes a luxury that we can no longer afford.

A new type of journal that begins to address this issue of multiple review has appeared over the past few years. *PLoS One* and its growing number of clones judge papers on their technical correctness, rather than on any attempt to evaluate appropriateness for the journal's audience, or impact.[6] The job of evaluating the importance of the research is seen as being that of the readers rather than the reviewers. Rather than asking 'Is this paper right for the journal?' referees are essentially asked 'Is this paper right?' This strips out the multiple submit-review-reject-resubmit loops, and so may go part of the way to reducing the costs of publication.

A concerted transition to OA may lead to significant reductions in the cost of journals. A significant move to the author-pays model (Gold OA) may offer an unprecedented opportunity to introduce market forces. At present libraries pay subscriptions to publishers, but researchers are frequently ignorant of the high cost of the journals they consult. Once they have to pay up front to publish their work, researchers will become aware of the comparative costs of Article Processing Charges (APCs) in different titles. (Although, if we are not careful about how we structure the payment of publication fees, we risk replacing the current failed subscription market with a failed OA market.)

Interdisciplinary and international research

One of the current fashions among research-funding bodies is to encourage interdisciplinary research. The belief is that major new breakthroughs will take place not necessarily by digging deeper and deeper into more and more narrow sub-disciplines, but by bringing together insights from different disciplines and encouraging cross-pollination of ideas and techniques. The traditional print journal does not encourage interdisciplinary research – it bundles together a group of similar papers into issues and volumes. As these bundles become larger and larger the journals may split into daughter journals – Parts A, B, C, ... – each daughter part more narrowly focused than the parent. In the days of journal browsing this gave readers the opportunity to gain a deep knowledge of their sub-field, but it does not encourage the acquisition of knowledge from beyond that field.

Today, browsing through journals is rarely the researcher's primary means of identifying articles. Most will start with a search of abstracting and indexing (A&I) services (perhaps the ultimate abstracting and indexing service, Google). These services begin to break down the physical and virtual boundaries of the journal and bring all papers of potential interest to the reader (assuming all the relevant journals are covered – gaps in coverage of A&I services being a topic for another paper).

This breaking down of barriers has implications for the library and its notion of 'the collection'. It has been noted that after moving to Big Deals institutions see a great deal of usage of journals not previously subscribed to. There are a number of reasons for this. First, no library could ever afford to subscribe to all titles it needed in order to satisfy the information needs of its users. There was always bound to be unmet demand. Second, the 'subscribed' titles today often reflect the holdings of ten years ago or more. The list of individual titles that a library would have subscribed to in the absence of the Big Deal would have changed over time. But it is also the case that even the most focused 'core collection' would always miss certain journals (and articles) likely to be of interest to researchers. This is especially true in interdisciplinary research. A library may have an excellent collection of surgery journals, but the key research insight may come from a paper published in a materials science journal.

PLoS One, described above, is beginning to move us away from the idea that papers need to be sorted into journals, and the idea of the journal as a discrete unit may be on the wane as *PLoS One* and its imitators continue to thrive and grow.

Large publishers would argue that by moving from subscribed titles to the Big Deal database sales models they are empowering interdisciplinary research. This is true, but the fear is that, as more libraries move away from Big Deals (as they slowly but surely are doing), we shall reduce the ability to carry out interdisciplinary research at the very moment that we wish to expand it.

There are similar arguments concerning collaborative research across institutional and national borders, again an area that receives attention from research funders and is heavily promoted. To be successful, researchers must be able to share research infrastructure. This may be elaborate, such as vastly expensive instrumentation (especially in high-energy physics and astronomy), through to the more prosaic internet and e-mail services. One part of the infrastructure is the research literature. At the moment, distribution of access to the research literature is highly skewed to the richer (mainly Western) countries, with good access in some poorly developed countries where publishers offer discretionary charity access (e.g., HINARI (Access to Research in Health Programme), AGORA (Access to Global Online Research in Agriculture), etc.). This highly skewed pattern is not conducive to good collaboration. It is harder for two people to work together as equals if one has access to a much greater range of the scholarly literature than does the other.

As we continue to see greater emphasis on cross-disciplinary and collaborative research, so the failings of the current communications systems will become more apparent and there will be greater pressure to revise how we communicate. OA will provide part of the solution, and it is interesting that in the fields dominated by the largest shared instrumentation (CERN for high-energy physics, telescopes for astronomy, etc.) we already have very popular and highly used OA solutions (arXiv, ADS, etc.). We also see this in biomedicine, where genetic resources (the human genome, protein structure databases, etc.) are made freely available.

Conclusion

Publication of research results has been an integral part of the research process for over 400 years. Journals have adapted to fulfil the evolving requirements placed upon them by the scholarly community and they continue to adapt as they find their place online. But journals have also, by their very nature, affected the research process and moulded the behaviour of researchers. This two-way interaction is set to continue as new technology and the shifting priorities of research funders allow new iterations of a centuries-old tradition.

References

1   Roosendaal, H. E., Geurts, P. A. Th. M. (1997) Forces and Functions in Scientific Communication: an analysis of their interplay. In: *Cooperative Research Information Systems in Physics, August 31–September 4, Oldenburg, Germany,* www.physik.uni-oldenburg.de/conferences/crisp97/roosendaal.html.

2   Garfield, E. *The Agony and the Ecstasy: the history and meaning of the journal impact factor,* www.psych.utoronto.ca/users/psy3001/files/JCR.pdf.

3   www.wellcome.ac.uk/stellent/groups/corporatesite/@policy_communications/documents/web_document/wtvm054838.pdf, p. 10.

4   www.ipo.gov.uk/ipreview-finalreport.pdf.

5   www.rin.ac.uk/our-work/communicating-and-disseminating-research/activities-costs-and-funding-flows-scholarly-commu.

6   www.plosone.org/static/information.action.

4

Creative communication in a 'publish or perish' culture: can postdocs lead the way?

Katie Anders and Liz Elvidge

ABSTRACT

Technological advancement has transformed research across the STEM (science, technology, engineering and mathematics) disciplines, leading to the development of new fields of enquiry, as well as novel research tools and methodologies. It has also generated a variety of original media for communicating scholarly research. Yet, despite this, articles in highly ranked, peer-reviewed journals remain — for better or worse — the panacea. Postdocs working at research-intensive universities are required to demonstrate innovation to further their careers. However, the pressure to publish in order to secure a permanent academic post means that the gap for creative research communication is narrow. Most postdocs are accordingly conservative in the way that they report and disseminate their research. This chapter looks at how the 'publish or perish' culture affects the ways postdocs understand and make choices about communicating their research. Using a recent public outreach project as a case study, it explores the benefits of participating in creative dissemination projects and discusses the broader value of creative forms of science communication.

Introduction

This chapter looks at the ways in which the 'publish or perish' culture which exists within STEM (science, technology, engineering and mathematics) disciplines influences the choices postdoctoral researchers (postdocs) make about how to conduct research and communicate their findings. Drawing on data examining the role of creativity in STEM research, it explores the scope for creative forms of research dissemination and suggests that while developing a strong portfolio of peer-reviewed publication is critical, more creative forms of scholarly communication are also of increasing value to postdocs' career progression.

Publishing in the digital age

Technological advancement has transformed research across the STEM disciplines, leading to the creation of new fields of enquiry and the growth of novel methodologies and research tools. It has also generated a variety of original media for sharing data and communicating findings. Yet despite this, articles in highly ranked, peer-reviewed journals remain – for better or worse – the panacea of scholarly communication.

Rather than transforming the way in which research is disseminated, the advent of digital technology seems, somewhat ironically, to have reinforced traditional modes of scholarly communication. Debate concerning the accessibility (or lack thereof) of online publications has led to the development of alternative communication strategies. These include Open Access journals, institutional repositories, pre-print servers, social networking sites and personal blogs.[1] At the same time, digital citation indices continue, despite debate regarding their usefulness,[2-4] to quantify the 'impact' of academic research and reinforce the hegemony of the traditional journal as the primary means of assessing academic standing.[5]

Academics' motivations for publishing are multiple, and include registering a claim to research, securing recognition and esteem from peers, reaching target audiences and responding to external pressures such as meeting the demands of funders and research assessment criteria.[6] But for the majority of postdocs working in research-intensive universities, the cultivation of a strong record of peer-reviewed publication is, first and foremost, imperative to securing a permanent academic post.[7-8]

Publish or perish: the struggle for innovation in a culture of 'impact'

For postdocs, competition for scarce resources – namely, research funding and academic posts – takes place in a context characterized by ambivalent goals. On the one hand, they must maximize opportunities to publish. On the other, many recognize that in order to distinguish themselves from their peers, they must also demonstrate a degree of innovation. As one postdoc explained:

> You don't get interesting results unless you are creative. You can follow the route that everyone does but you don't stand out. You're just one of the 10,000 people who work in science. You're nothing special.[9]

This drive for creativity is substantiated by policy which charges research institutions with the task of producing innovative thinkers to fuel the knowledge economy.[10] But researchers' ability to exercise creativity is stymied by separate policy which promotes the production of knowledge that is deemed to have social and economic relevance, or impact.[11–12] Prioritizing the impact of academic endeavour over its originality is, it is argued, having a 'deadening effect' on researchers' ability to be creative[13] by focusing attention – and funding – on intellectual activity that is likely to generate socially relevant results, as opposed to 'blue skies' projects with less predictable outcomes.[14] In this confused context, balancing creativity and productivity within the timescale of a short-term contract can feel like something of a high-wire act. As one postdoc described:

> If you're not seen to be creative and driving ideas forward, there's very little point in even writing an application ... but it's very difficult to balance what you want to do creatively with actually having a job and getting funded.[15]

Despite the impetus to innovate, research suggests that postdocs tend to follow disciplinary norms, making conservative decisions about how to conduct research and adopting correspondingly risk-averse strategies for reporting and communicating it. In the largest and most recent study of its kind, researchers in the USA discovered 'no evidence' that postdocs were vetoing traditional research and publishing practices in favour of newer approaches. Conversely, 'as arguably the most vulnerable populations in the scholarly community', they were found to be the group of researchers most likely to 'hew the norms' of their chosen discipline.[16]

In the UK, meeting the requirements of the Research Excellence Framework or REF (formerly RAE, Research Assessment Exercise) is a priority for all academics, and one which provides a strong disincentive for communicating research via non-traditional – and particularly non peer-reviewed – media.[17] A recent study found that 'creative' forms of dissemination were perceived as either 'not important' or 'not applicable' to 95% of medical and biological scientists, 98% of physical scientists and mathematicians and 83% of engineers and computer scientists. 'Other' forms of communication, including seminars, workshops, user groups and public-speaking events, were perceived as either 'not important' or 'not applicable' to 90% of medical and biological scientists, 96% of physical scientists and mathematicians and 92% of engineers and computer scientists.[18]

Speaking to postdocs about creativity, it becomes clear that many understand that it should play a central role in their research. Terms such as 'innovative' and 'original' remain measures of significant esteem and recur throughout postdocs' narratives. However, the choices that postdocs make about how to employ creativity seem to be adversely influenced by the 'publish or perish' culture in a number of significant ways.

First, postdocs frequently demonstrate conservatism in their research strategy; that is, when choosing what to research, and how. Many tend to choose 'safe' projects, with a high probability of generating positive, publishable results. They also tend to focus on the stated objectives of the projects that they are involved in, as opposed to spending time and resources in pursuing new and interesting, but potentially time-consuming, findings which might arise in the course of their research. As one researcher stated:

> You have to produce results constantly and the way most universities see your results is by publication, and you can't publish negative results – or you can, but you can never publish negative results in good journals. So you have to have things that work. They aren't necessarily the most creative things.[19]

Postdocs employ similarly risk-averse strategies when writing and disseminating their research, where many report deferring discussion of interesting new methodologies, methods and even findings which might have arisen in the course of their research. Speaking of the rigours of science communication, one postdoc said:

I think they would like to see people who always look a bit further than the conventional methods but I wonder ... if they'd like to see me be very creative? Maybe they would like it a bit more if I was using solid things they know have been tested for a long time. Because my field is so new, I think they are a bit sceptical, so I think they would prefer it if I say 'well, this method already worked in biology'.[20]

Finally, postdocs generally choose traditional methods of research communication, focusing on publishing articles in highly ranked journals and presenting papers and posters at prestigious international conferences. As one postdoc explained:

We tend to turn to very conventional methods; nice graphs and pictures and tables or put it all on a poster or in a very well structured talk, and I see no creativity there at all.[21]

These narratives demonstrate that some postdocs, at least, feel a level of frustration that their scientific curiosity and creativity is curtailed both by the imperative to focus on generating publications and by the rigorous and restrictive format of the journal article. One postdoc explained that even though they feel that their work is creative, it can be made to feel uncreative when disseminated in this way:

I think my work is creative but I don't present it as being creative ... I think science is quite rigorous, so when you present your results ... you present the robustness of your data and therefore it doesn't feel very creative ... things that get put into papers and publications tend to be the cold, hard facts. Because it's demonstrating the cold, hard facts, the creative side tends to get hidden quite a lot.[9]

The attitudes and advice of postdocs' PIs (principal investigators) appear to play a role in reinforcing this conservatism. Research indicates that some postdocs are actively discouraged by their PIs from spending time on creative research and dissemination and are advised to focus, instead, on 'publishing in the right venues'.[16] Interviews with postdocs and PIs substantiate this. Many postdocs, while not openly discouraged from participating in creative research and dissemination, stated that their PIs viewed such undertakings as a distraction. Interviews with PIs further suggested that even those who actively encourage their postdocs to be creative are pragmatic in their assessment of the need to balance such activity with producing publications:

> I at least try to encourage them to be as daring as possible. You need to, in the present environment, you need to spit out a paper once in a while. It doesn't have to be the most ingenious, but you need it otherwise you'll just leave. Some people … feel this is against the entire ethos of academia. That's admirable, but not very practical for your progression.[22]

Creative communication: can postdocs lead the way?

Despite the general reluctance to use non-traditional forms of scholarly communication, a number of projects led by postdocs are being developed with the purpose of communicating the findings of STEM research in original and creative ways. One of these is the Beautiful Science project, which has been developed by postdocs at Imperial College, London. Beautiful Science teams 15 postdocs in STEM disciplines with artists who collaborate to produce visual representations of scientific research taking place at Imperial. The pieces are produced over time, then communicated and discussed at a gallery exhibition and a series of workshops, road shows and discussion events.

Beautiful Science targets multiple audiences. It represents a form of scholarly communication that participants hope can prompt fellow scientists to conceptualize and discuss their research in alternative ways. It also aims to engage and excite a more general audience by communicating complex scientific processes and findings using widely accessible media, while revealing something of the creative side of scientific enterprise.

Given the culture of conservatism that influences most postdocs to disseminate their research via traditional media, it's worth exploring both the motivations of those who devote time and energy to communicating their scientific research in this way, and the value of such projects for postdocs' career progression.

A primary motivation for postdocs' participation in Beautiful Science is that it constitutes a more broadly structured medium for sharing and discussing research: one that provides space to communicate ideas and information in an open and creative way. This gives researchers an opportunity to explore and discuss aspects of their work which they find interesting, exciting or simply 'beautiful', but which cannot be routinely communicated to their peers in a journal article. As one postdoc explained:

> A journal is very, very formal. You have to give precise information. Whereas with this you don't, you can create more speculation. You can still discuss a hypothesis but you can use a different language.[23]

Another significant reason why postdocs participate in this type of project is that it provides an opportunity to communicate to non-scientists something of the process, purpose and potential impact of the science that they are involved in. Some feel that this is important to debunk the myth of the scientist in a lab coat 'doing mysterious things and not really contributing anything useful to society' and to combat poor science communication by providing accurate, accessible information.[24] For others, projects like Beautiful Science are a platform to engage with non-scientists and inspire a new generation of potential scientists. In both cases, the ability to communicate research and demonstrate its value is of paramount importance.

Taking part in civic engagement is increasingly advantageous for postdocs, both for their research and for their career progression. Those who design and lead such projects acquire a number of valuable transferable skills, including project and people management, events organization and experience in writing grant applications and obtaining sponsorship. Those who participate gain valuable experience of communicating to a non-scientific audience.

Doing this effectively requires researchers to reflect upon and clarify their ideas before communicating them in 'plain language' or, in the case of Beautiful Science, via artistic representations. Some postdocs have reported that this process encourages a reflexivity that helps to bring fresh perspectives to their research:

> It opens your mind ... I never realised how just a very simple concept can be explained in plain language. So, this opens your mind. It also helps you to slow down and understand what you are doing, and I think that helped me in the last part of my postdoc.[25]

But the ability to communicate science is also of significant value to postdocs as they begin to apply for research funding. Many grant applicants are now required as part of the funding application process to set out the contribution they anticipate making to society. Participating in this type of dissemination provides experience in explaining research in layman's terms, which many postdocs do not otherwise acquire during the course of their short-term contract:

> Funders need somebody who is able to communicate properly to the public to say 'we are doing something that is good for society'. So it's important ... I have been involved in writing my own grants and ... it was difficult because you are not used to using that language ... not all scientists are good speakers, so I think you need to be able to have the tools, or the training or the inspiration from other people like artists, to explain those things.[23]

This narrative illustrates an important point: that a policy of re-conceptualizing the 'impact' of research to include a socio-economic dimension has brought with it a new communication strategy. In order to justify the cost to the taxpayer of publicly funded research, scientists are increasingly required to explain the impact of their research in ways which can be felt and understood outside the academy.

The imperative to communicate 'impact' represents a departure from traditional scholarly communication and, indeed, serves an entirely different function. Although civic engagement is far from critical to postdocs' career progression, research councils, independent funding bodies and (consequently) academic institutions are taking a greater interest in this form of communication. It is common now for universities specializing in STEM disciplines to formulate and publicize a civic engagement strategy. Funders ring-fence money for science communication and public outreach initiatives, and professional bodies award prizes for outstanding civic engagement. The European Commission's Descartes Prize for Excellence in Science Communication and the Royal Society's Michael Faraday Award for Communicating Science to a UK Audience represent two notable examples of this.

Because of this shift in the way that civic engagement is viewed, more and more projects that communicate science to the public are being devised and funded. Many of these are conceived and managed by postdocs. The Beautiful Science project is one example, supported by a grant from the Wellcome Trust under the auspices of its People's Award.

For postdocs who disseminate their research in non-traditional ways, publishing remains a priority. But participation in civic engagement provides an important outlet for creativity, a new language with which to discuss research with peers and a platform for reaching a broader audience and informing popular discussion about important scientific issues.[26–27] It also equips postdocs with skills and experience that will prove increasingly advantageous when they apply for independent research funding and permanent academic (and non-academic) posts.

Conclusion

Despite the growing importance of communicating scientific research to a general audience, and the benefits of learning to do so, participation in civic engagement and other forms of creative dissemination is still largely overlooked within traditional academic reward systems. What incentives there are remain 'weak and indirect',[28] and take-up is consequently low.

There is, however, reason for cautious optimism. Cultural change, albeit slow, has been demonstrated both at a policy level, where funding for civic engagement is being allocated, and at the grass roots, where small groups of committed postdocs and other academics are taking advantage of available resources to develop creative dissemination projects. But there are also suggestions that these changes may be filtering into departmental culture. While it has been shown that PIs display a general antipathy toward projects that take time and energy away from the core tasks of research, such attitudes are not universal. One of the founders of Beautiful Science reported that they received enthusiastic support from their manager when the project was introduced and explained to them. The fact that by then Beautiful Science had met with considerable success – and financial support – is sure to have helped. Nonetheless, this reception demonstrates recognition, at a managerial level, of the value of creative dissemination projects, both to the postdocs involved and to the academic departments and institutions that gain funding and positive publicity from them.

For such enterprises to flourish, it is vital that research councils and other funding bodies continue to support them, and for academic institutions to recognize those who lead and participate in them. It is also important that graduate students and postdocs be taught that civic engagement is now part of the role of a conscientious scientist.[27] Most importantly, academic reward systems must begin to take account of the value of civic engagement, and other forms of creative dissemination, and to support and incentivize academics' efforts to engage with the public. Unless and until this takes place, such activity will remain peripheral as postdocs continue to publish or perish.

Acknowledgement

This chapter was written using semi-structured interview data collected from postdocs and principal investigators at a research-intensive UK university. Research was undertaken for the Vitae Innovate Project conducted by Elaine Walsh, Katie Anders and Liz Elvidge in 2010. For more information about this project, please visit: www3.imperial.ac.uk/staffdevelopment/postdocs1/projects/innovate.

The chapter also includes original data from semi-structured interviews with project managers and participants of the Beautiful Science project at Imperial College, London. For more information about Beautiful Science, please visit: www.beautifulscience.info/.

References

1   *CT Watch Quarterly* (2007) The Coming Revolution in Scholarly Communications and Cyberinfrastructure, *CT Watch Quarterly*, **3** (3).
2   Altbach, P. (2006) The Tyranny of Citations, *Inside Higher Education*, (8 May).
3   Brown, H. (2007) How Impact Factors Changed Medical Publishing – and Science, *British Medical Journal*, **334** (7593), 561–4.
4   Williams, G. (2007) Should We Ditch Impact Factors?, *British Medical Journal*, **334** (7593), 598.
5   Ayers, L. and Grisham, C. (2003) Why IT Has Not Paid Off as We Had Hoped (Yet), *EDUCAUSE Review*, **38** (6), 40–51.
6   Research Information Network (2009) *Communicating Knowledge: how and why UK researchers publish and disseminate their findings*, Final Report, www.jisc.ac.uk/publications/research/2009/communicatingknowledgereport.aspx.
7   Larkin, M. J. (1999) Pressure to Publish Stifles Young Talent, *Nature*, **397**,

467, www.nature.com/nature/journal/v397/n6719/full/397467a0.html.

8 Archer, L. (2008) Younger Academics' Constructions of 'Authenticity', 'Success' and Professional Identity, *Studies in Higher Education*, **33** (4), 385–403.

9 Postdoc, participant 20. Primary interview transcripts. Interviewed by Anders, K., August 2010.

10 League of European Research Universities (2010) *Doctoral Degrees beyond 2010: training talented researchers for society*, www.leru.org/files/publications/ LERU_Doctoral_degrees_beyond_2010.pdf.

11 Ozga, J. (1998) The Entrepreneurial Researcher: re-formations of identity in the research marketplace, *International Studies in Sociology of Education*, **8**, 143–54.

12 Harris, S. (2005) Rethinking Academic Identities in Neo-liberal Times, *Teaching in Higher Education*, **10**, 421–33.

13 Atwood, R. (2010) Impact's Impact Could Be the Stifling of New Ideas, *Times Higher Education*, (6 May).

14 Walsh, E., Anders, K., Handcock, S. and Elvidge, E. (2011) Reclaiming Creativity in an Era of Impact: exploring ideas about creative research in science and engineering, *Studies in Higher Education*, (October), www.tandfonline.com/doi/abs/10.1080/03075079.2011.620091.

15 Postdoc, participant 24. Primary interview transcripts. Interviewed by Anders, K., July 2010.

16 Harley, D., Krzys Acord, S., Earl-Novel, S., Lawrence, S. and King, J. (2010) *Final Report: assessing the future landscape of scholarly communication: an exploration of faculty values and needs in seven disciplines*, http://escholarship.org/uc/cshe_fsc.

17 Research Information Network (2009) *Communicating Knowledge: how and why UK researchers publish and disseminate their findings*, www.jisc.ac.uk/publications/ research/2009/communicatingknowledgereport.aspx.

18 Research Information Network (2009) *Communicating Knowledge: how and why UK researchers publish and disseminate their findings. Supporting paper 3: Report and analysis of researcher survey*, www.jisc.ac.uk/publications/research/2009/ communicatingknowledgereport.aspx.

19 Postdoc, participant 25. Primary interview transcripts. Interviewed by Anders, K., August 2010.

20 Postdoc, participant 23. Primary interview transcripts. Interviewed by Anders, K., July 2010.

21 Postdoc, participant 17. Primary interview transcripts. Interviewed by Anders, K., July 2010.

22 Principal Investigator, participant 26. Primary interview transcripts. Interviewed by Anders, K., August 2010.

23 Beautiful Science participant 'S'. Primary interview transcripts. Interviewed by Anders, K., March 2012.

24 Beautiful Science participant 'R'. Primary interview transcripts. Interviewed by Anders, K., March 2012.

25 Beautiful Science participant 'H'. Primary interview transcripts. Interviewed by Anders, K., March 2012.

26 Friedman, D. (2008) Public Outreach: a scientific imperative, *The Journal of Neuroscience*, **28** (46), 11745–54.

27 Leshner, A. (2007) Outreach Training Needed, *Science Magazine*, **315** (5809), 161.

28 Research Information Network and British Library (2009) *Patterns of Information Use and Exchange: case studies of researchers in the life sciences. Briefing,* www.rin.ac.uk/our-work/using-and-accessing-information-resources/patterns-information-use-and-exchange-case-studies.

5

Cybertaxonomy

Vincent S. Smith

ABSTRACT

The way taxonomic information is created, tested, accessed, thought about and used is changing dramatically with the application of information and communications technologies (ICTs). This cyber-enabled taxonomy is not only changing the efficiency and work practices of taxonomists, but also changing ways of disseminating taxonomic data, and, arguably, the very nature of taxonomic knowledge. In this chapter I examine some of the major outputs of taxonomic research; how ICTs are affecting their production, dissemination and reuse; and common impediments to further progress, including a lack of incentives to build, sustain and populate appropriate infrastructures.

Introduction

Biological taxonomy and systematics is one of the oldest scientific disciplines. It aims to explore, discover, characterize, name and classify species; to study their evolutionary relationships; and to map their geographic distributions and ecological associations. Taxonomy draws on information from many disciplines in order to build a coherent picture of the extent and trajectory of life on earth. This is currently enshrined in an estimated 5.4 million volumes (circa 800,000 monographs and 40,000 journal titles) published on natural history since 1469.[1]

Cybertaxonomy is a contraction of 'cyber-enabled taxonomy' and involves the application of information and communications technologies (ICTs) to taxonomy.[2] It shares the traditional goals of taxonomy but uses non-traditional hardware, software, instrumentation, communication tools and work practices, bringing information science and technologies to bear on the data and information generated by the study of organisms, their genes and their interactions.

In this short review I highlight areas where cybertaxonomy is transforming taxonomic practice, particularly in the collection, management, synthesis and dissemination of taxonomic works. This transformation has the potential to provide unprecedented global access to information on biological species and their role in nature. The full realization of this potential requires a number of further technical advances, where progress is being made; but also cultural change, where progress may be harder to achieve.

Taxonomic names and checklists

The names by which organisms are known are the basis for communication about them. Almost all information relating to organisms is given context by scientific names. When due allowance is made for problems such as homonymy, synonymy, orthographic variation and the dynamic relationships of names (as text character strings) and concepts (sets of organisms represented by names), names offer a near-comprehensive system of metadata by which to index and organize biodiversity information.[3] Thus taxonomic names are, in theory, unique identifiers that unambiguously link past and present-day references to all organisms, enabling all biologists talking about an organism to be sure that they are talking about the same thing. This fact may seem trivial and rather mundane, but the technical and social challenges of electronically recording and disseminating names and their concepts, coupled with the associated challenges of aggregating this information, mean that the taxonomic community is still far from being able to achieve simple goals like compiling a list of all known species, or more selective lists for regional, ecological or functional habitats.

The form of binomial scientific names that we use today was invented by the Swedish botanist Carl von Liné (Carolus Linnaeus). His system of nomenclature latterly became incorporated into a series of nomenclatural codes, currently regulated by three principal authorities, governing plants,[4] bacteria[5] and animals.[6] These codes are not legally enforceable, but provide a social construct that is almost universally recognized under which nomenclatural acts (i.e., all matters affecting names) are performed.

A central tenet of each code is a requirement to publish formally all nomenclatural acts. Traditionally, publication had to be on paper-based media so that it could be preserved in print-holding libraries. Calls to improve access have led the botanical community to accept web-based (electronic-only) publication of plant names from 1 January 2012.[7] The zoological community is likely to follow suit[8] for animal names, and these acts will significantly help to improve access to taxonomic research. However, electronic publication itself does little to address the fragmentation of information contained within these papers. In fact, electronic-only publication of nomenclature risks significantly increasing the fragmentation of taxonomy, because of the relative ease of establishing electronic-only journals.

At present some 15,000–20,000 new species descriptions and thousands of other nomenclatural acts governed by the codes are published annually.[9] Historically, these types of papers have been published across an estimated 40,000 journal titles,[1] although only a few thousand of these journals are currently in print. Many have limited distribution in a handful of specialist libraries, and of those available electronically, a majority have restricted access behind publishers' pay-walls.

In order to bring together thematic collections of papers, specialist taxonomists have increasingly used ICTs to collaborate in compiling taxon-centric databases citing published nomenclatural acts relevant to higher taxa. Countless such databases are now accessible on the web, with some supporting online editing. Some of the largest, like LepIndex[10] and the Diptera Database,[11] focus on the major insect groups. Together, these two databases alone cover almost half a million species of butterflies, moths and flies (nearly 25% of all currently described biota).

As technical barriers to databasing have fallen, smaller efforts covering more obscure taxa have developed. Increasingly these are being integrated with larger efforts in order to compile more comprehensive and up-to-date taxonomic resources. Some of the largest, such as the International Plant Names Index (www.ipni.org), serve simply to aggregate names and bibliographic data, without reference to an overarching biological classification. Others, like Species 2000 (www.sp2000.org), have sought to compile full biological classifications. Some are regional lists, such as Fauna Europaea (www.faunaeur.org), while others, like the World Register of Marine Species (www.marinespecies.org), cover specific habitats.[12]

Unfortunately, these integrative taxonomic checklists suffer from two major problems. First, as the distance between the source contributor and the aggregating publisher grows, it becomes harder to maintain the frequency of updates and engagement necessary to assure the quality of the final product. Second, these initiatives find it difficult to accommodate more than one taxonomic 'view' or classification scheme.[13] These challenges seriously limit the ability of checklists to reflect the dynamic nature of taxonomic nomenclature and concepts. A major international effort is therefore underway (globalnames.org) to model all taxonomic names and concepts and to link them to multiple classifications. The foundation for this effort is the ZooBank database (zoobank.org), a community-led effort to compile zoological nomenclatural information in order to ease the transition into electronic-only publications.

Species descriptions

Natural history libraries and museums collectively hold most of the world's published knowledge on biological diversity. These collections are of exceptional value because taxonomy depends – more than any other natural science – upon historic literature. The cited 'half-life' of taxonomic literature is longer than that of any other scientific domain, and the rate at which it becomes irrelevant is much slower than that of other fields.[1] In order positively to identify a rare specimen, a biologist may have to consult a 100-year-old text, because that was the last time the organism was found, recorded and described. However, early literature is often rare, with very limited distribution across the globe; and access to library and museum collections is difficult for most people.

In an effort to address these problems the major taxonomic libraries worldwide joined forces through the Biodiversity Heritage Library (BHL) project to co-ordinate the digitization of their vast catalogues of taxonomic literature. Optical Character Recognition (OCR) techniques are applied to extract textual information that is then indexed in order to help users find literature relevant to their research interests through a central portal (www.biodiversitylibrary.org). To date, the BHL has scanned over 39 million pages of natural history text. Most of this literature predates 1923, because these works are considered public domain under US copyright law. Unfortunately, at least 50% of all species have been described after 1923, and these works are protected by copyright. Digitizing in-copyright works requires lengthy and expensive negotiation with the rights-holders before the works can be incorporated as part of the BHL portal. Furthermore, BHL largely excludes non-English language literature, although an increasing number of subsidiary projects have now been initiated to digitize European, Arabic and Chinese-language publications.

Although most in-copyright literature is not widely accessible, other developments are helping to improve access. In recent years *ZooTaxa*, the largest single taxonomic journal, publishing 18–24% of all animal species descriptions,[9] has provided an Open Access track for articles. Many professional taxonomists from developed countries who have funds to meet publication charges have thus enjoyed greater exposure for their work; but those without access to such funds can meet publication charges only from their own pockets. One solution has been to exploit efficiencies in the publication process so that publishers can dramatically lower their charges. This is one of the models adopted by Pensoft (www.pensoft.net), a specialist taxonomic publisher based in Eastern Europe. Pensoft's low cost base, coupled with its efficient publication workflow that automatically 'marks up' published papers, keeps its publication charges very low. This mark-up adds machine-readable structure that facilitates greater reuse of species descriptions and their underlying data.[14] Species descriptions published by Pensoft are pushed, on publication, to aggregators such as the web-based Encyclopedia of Life project (eol.org), while taxonomic names and specimen records are automatically extracted and pushed to appropriate public repositories like ZooBank and the Global Biodiversity Information Facility (www.gbif.org).

Arguably, the ultimate efficiency in producing taxonomic species descriptions is the automated generation of a publication from the underlying images, character data and specimen data compiled during the researchers' investigations. Because taxonomic information is highly structured, and in many cases standardized, it is possible automatically to construct formal species descriptions from an underlying database of information. This functionality is supported in the DELTA software package,[15] which allows users to build natural-language descriptions of species and identification keys from an underlying matrix of character data. DELTA highlights the efficiencies of structuring data for reuse. Similar functionality is being built into virtual research environments specifically developed for taxonomists.[14] These systems facilitate semi-automated construction of full species descriptions via a series of workflows embedded into web-based software. They allow users to collaborate with colleagues in order to construct taxonomic manuscripts from an underlying database of taxonomic data on the web. Users can preview their paper as it would look in a journal and then submit it for peer review, without having to go to the publisher's website. This approach, combined with the powerful descriptive functionality of software like DELTA, has the potential dramatically to improve the efficiency of constructing and publishing species descriptions.

Evolutionary trees (phylogeny)

Phylogenetics is the study of evolutionary relationships among groups of organisms, which are largely discovered through molecular sequence data and morphological data matrices. Although Linnaean taxonomy is methodologically and logically distinct from phylogeny, taxonomic classifications are richly informed by phylogenetic analysis, which provides the framework across which taxonomies can be refined, allowing biologists to explain and predict ecological functions. Closely related species frequently share, for example, similar food sources, reproductive strategies, physiologies and behaviours.

Phylogenetic analysis can be extremely computationally intensive. Although advances in computer processing power, coupled with more efficient algorithms, have radically reduced the time taken to produce equivalent phylogenetic hypotheses, comparable advances have resulted in more taxon- and character-rich matrices that form the basis for these analyses. This means that a state-of-the-art phylogeny produced today is, arguably, just as time-consuming to compute as it was ten years ago.

ICTs have had a profound impact on how we display phylogenetic trees.[16] Trees are relatively simple structures, but, as the size of phylogenies has grown, it has become difficult to accommodate them within the confines of the printed page, or even of a computer screen. The 2003 special issue of *Science* devoted to the tree of life[17] included a 3000-taxa tree that was 'best viewed when enlarged to a 1.5-meter diameter'. Today, phylogenies with tens of thousands of taxa are being published[18] and the problem of visualizing phylogenies is becoming harder as increasing computing power enables researchers to construct ever-larger trees. Computing technology is enabling novel visualizations, ranging from geophylogenies embedded on digital globes, to touch-screen interfaces that enable greater interaction with evolutionary trees. These interfaces expand the explanatory power of phylogenies, allowing topologies to be cross-referenced in a multitude of ways.

The increasing availability of georeferencing services[19] and georeferenced DNA sequences[20] means that geophylogenies – using latitude and longitude to locate the tips of a tree on a sphere representing the Earth – are increasingly being used in phylogeny visualization. Google Earth's ability to display time-series data means that spatial and temporal data can be combined to create compelling visualizations, such as of the spread of zoonotic viruses.[21–2] Touch-screen interfaces offer potential for enabling interactions between researchers.[23] Although phylogenetic software developers have yet to exploit fully the possibilities of these devices, they offer a tantalizing glimpse of the future of managing very large trees.

Biological collections

Usually information can be extracted from natural history collections only by visiting the host institution. Name-bearing type specimens are among the most important items within these institutions, as they are the basis on which taxonomic identification and descriptions are made. Every specimen carries with it a wealth of information about its identification and provenance in space and time. These data are the foundation for further research, and also essential to meeting a broad cascade of policy obligations and commitments that require accurate information about the identification and location of species. The EU Habitats Directive, the Global Strategy for Plant Conservation and the Convention on International Trade in Endangered Species (CITES) are just some of the treaties and frameworks that require detailed information derived from natural history collections. It is estimated that there are as many as 2–3 billion specimens in these collections worldwide.[2] A small but growing proportion of these specimens lie in a state of transition as digital representations and associated metadata are captured to facilitate new ways to access, integrate and use natural history collections.

Virtual collections make it possible for digital surrogates of specimens to be provided to anyone via the web, rather than requiring expensive physical visits to collections or incurring the risks and expense of sending valuable and fragile specimens via mail. Although digital surrogates are not always satisfactory substitutes for physical specimens, they are often sufficient to make taxonomic decisions, particularly when two-dimensional images are adequate to capture most of the salient features necessary to identify organisms, such as botanical specimens mounted on card, or butterflies and moths, which are normally pinned flat.

The major barrier to digitizing museum specimens is the sheer scale of the task. For example, the Natural History Museum, London has some 70 million specimens, many of them complex and fragile. Until recently, digitization efforts have usually focused on the tiny proportion of specimens with an applied commercial, medical or veterinary use, or with a significant cultural or historical value. Recent advances in technology, coupled with rapid workflows, have made more comprehensive programmes possible.[24] Activities such as the €13 million mass digitization programme at NCB Naturalis in Leiden,[25] covering 7–8 million specimens in detail and a further 30 million objects at lower resolution, illustrate that major efficiency gains can be made when working at scale: the larger a digitization project becomes, the lower the unit cost per specimen.

Most current large-scale digitization programmes focus on two-dimensional representations of specimens, but for some material there is a need to capture other dimensions. For example, a wide variety of Computer Tomography (CT) techniques are now used to obtain cross-sections, which can be combined into virtual models of a specimen without damaging the original. This approach is particularly suited to paleontological material, where a matrix of surrounding rock may obscure much of a specimen. For some organisms, like protists, videos of live specimens are more effective, since physical specimens cannot be readily stored using conventional curatorial methods. In other cases images may have little value, but a specimen's metadata is its greatest asset. This particularly applies to mineralogical specimens, where mining and resource industries are interested in the chemical analysis data associated with mineral samples and the geological context in which samples are found.

As digital natural history archives grow, it has become crucial to create repositories and portals to store, manage and access this information. Morphbank (www.morphbank.net) is one example of an online repository of images for natural history specimens. Some major

European collections have used the Europeana portal (www.europeana. eu/portal) to facilitate integration of digital collections. Another approach adopted by the Global Plants Initiative was to use JSTOR (plants.jstor.org), a not-for-profit initiative creating digital archives of scholarly resources.

Digital collections have created a new set of research possibilities. In some cases digital surrogates of specimens have been mobilized on the web to engage a much larger pool of people with the task of transcribing specimen label metadata. This is illustrated by the Herbarium@home project (herbariaunited.org/atHome) which crowdsources the task of capturing plant label information from digital photos, so as to collect structured textual data rapidly. Pools of online specimen pictures also facilitate more rapid identification of species. One novel application in this regard is DAISY,[26] the Digital Automated Identification SYstem. This compares digital photographs of insect morphological features with a database of shapes and markings gathered from image galleries of previously identified species. This works in much the same way as detectives use forensic databases to match crime-scene fingerprints or a suspect's face from security cameras. To be effective, DAISY requires a large reference set of previously identified specimens, and, although the project is still experimental, it highlights the value of comprehensively digitized collections. Another use for these collections is in the emerging field of telemicroscopy. This allows real-time microscope video to be shared with users over the web, and has been adapted for use by quarantine services and wildlife trade personnel,[2] linking them to museum specialists and their reference collections.

Conclusion: future challenges for taxonomy

The accelerating growth of data and knowledge in taxonomy is indisputable, but information still remains scattered, poorly documented and in formats that impede discovery and integration. The greatest challenge lies in pulling together these resources in data services to create a linked system of all taxonomic and evolutionary data, information and knowledge organized around biological taxonomies and phylogenies.[27] Using such a framework, one could compute scores on how much, and what kind of, information is available for any particular taxon and its relatives, generating new questions for further study. It would be possible to test and deploy new algorithmic approaches to understand better the causes and consequences of species diversification, the evolution of particular traits and the changing distribution of species over space and time. It might even be possible to develop large-scale standing analyses that alert researchers to new evidence that challenges existing knowledge, indicating where research is needed. Such an integrated framework would not only support a vibrant science, but also provide a mechanism for community cohesion and for clear messages about the central importance of taxonomy on a rapidly changing planet.

The Encyclopedia of Life (EOL) project (eol.org) is an example of a web-based portal that offers some of this functionality. EOL integrates diverse sources of taxonomic and evolutionary information in order to construct an authoritative series of web pages for all known species. Information is carefully sourced by curators who control its quality and provenance. Central to this development are associated tools that support the more local aggregation and development of specialist taxonomic information among researchers working within expert communities.[28] The Scratchpad project[29] is an example of such an activity supporting the local aggregation of data through a flexible system that allows people to create their own virtual research environments supporting their taxonomic activities. By embedding the process of taxonomic data creation, archival publication and scholarly publication into a website owned and managed by the contributing community, contributors can create specialist taxonomic resources that support their local needs. As of August 2012 an ecosystem of more than 450 Scratchpads is in operation, with a combined workforce of more than 6500 active contributors. Each Scratchpad is dedicated to one of a multitude of specialist taxonomic projects supporting more granular and regular contributions of taxonomic data than could be published through conventional publishing systems.[30] Tools like the Scratchpads, supporting the entire lifecycle of the scholarly communication process from data production to synthetic analysis and publication, have the potential completely to replace the traditional existing scholarly communication process for taxonomy.

References

1   Rinaldo, C. and Norton, C. (2009) BHL. The Biodiversity Heritage Library: an expanding international collaboration, *Nature Precedings*. doi:10.1038/npre.2009.3620.1.

2 Wheeler, Q. and Valdecasas, A. G. (2010) Cybertaxonomy and Ecology, *Nature Education Knowledge*, **1** (11), 6.

3 Page, R. D. M. (2008) Biodiversity Informatics: the challenge of linking data and the role of shared identifiers, *Briefings in Bioinformatics*, **9** (5), 345–54.

4 McNeill, J. et al. (2006) *International Code of Botanical Nomenclature (Vienna Code) adopted by the Seventeenth International Botanical Congress, Vienna, Austria, July 2005*, International Association for Plant Taxonomy.

5 Lapage, S. P. et al. (eds) (1992) *International Code of Nomenclature of Bacteria: Bacteriological Code, 1990 Revision*, ASM Press.

6 International Commission on Zoological Nomenclature (ICZN) (1999), *The International Code of Zoological Nomenclature*, The International Trust for Zoological Nomenclature.

7 Knapp, S., McNeill, J. and Turland, N. (2011) Changes to Publication Requirements Made at the XVIII International Botanical Congress in Melbourne – What Does E-publication Mean for You? *BMC Evolutionary Biology*, **11**, 251.

8 Knapp, S. and Wright, D. (2010) E-publish or Perish? In: Polaszek, A. (ed.) *Systema Naturae 250 – The Linnaean Ark*, CRC Press. doi: 10.1201/EBK1420095012-c8.

9 Zhang, Z. Q. (2011) Describing Unexplored Biodiversity: zootaxa in the International Year of Biodiversity, *Zootaxa*, **4**, 1–4.

10 Beccaloni, G. et al. (2003) *The Global Lepidoptera Names Index* (LepIndex), www.nhm.ac.uk/research-curation/research/projects/lepindex/.

11 Pape, T. and Thompson, F. C. (2012) *Systema Dipterorum*, www.diptera.org/.

12 Appeltans, W. et al. (2012) *World Register of Marine Species*, www.marinespecies.org/.

13 Pyle, R. L. (2004) Taxonomer: a relational data model for managing information relevant to taxonomic research, *PhyloInformatics*, **1**, 1–54.

14 Blagoderov, V. et al. (2010) Streamlining Taxonomic Publication: a working example with Scratchpads and ZooKeys, *ZooKeys*, **28**, 17–28.

15 Dallwitz, M. J. (1980) A General System for Coding Taxonomic Descriptions, *Taxon*, **21**, 41–6.

16 Page, R. D. M. (2012) Space, Time, Form: viewing the tree of life, *Trends in Ecology and Evolution*, **27**, 113–20.

17 Pennisi, E. (2003) Modernizing the Tree of Life, *Science*, **300**, 1692–7.

18 Goloboff, P. A. et al. (2009) Phylogenetic Analysis of 73 060 Taxa Corroborates Major Eukaryotic Groups, *Cladistics*, **25**, 211–30.

19 Hill, A. W. et al. (2009) Location, Location, Location: utilizing pipelines and services to more effectively georeference the world's biodiversity data, *BMC Bioinformatics*, **10** (Suppl. 1), S3.

20 Ausubel, J. H. (2009) A Botanical Macroscope, *Proceedings of the National Academy of Sciences of the United States of America*, **106**, 12569–70.

21 Lemey, P., Suchard, M. and Rambaut, A. (2009) Reconstructing the Initial Global Spread of a Human Influenza Pandemic: a Bayesian spatial-temporal model for the global spread of H1N1pdm, *PLoS Currents*, **1**, RRN1031.

22 Janies D et al. (2007) Genomic Analysis and Geographic Visualization of the Spread of Avian Influenza (H5N1), *Systematic Biology*, **56**, 321–9.

23 Isenberg, P. and Carpendale, S. (2007) Interactive Tree Comparison for Co-located Collaborative Information Visualization, *IEEE Transactions on Visualization and Computer Graphics*, **13**, 1232–9.

24 Smith, V. S. and Blagodero, V. (2012) Bringing Collections out of the Dark, *ZooKeys*, **209**, 1–6. doi: 10.3897/zookeys.209.3699.

25 van den Oever, J. P. and Gofferje, M. (2012) From Pilot to Production: large scale digitisation project at Naturalis Biodiversity Center. In: Blagoderov, V. and Smith, V. S. (eds) No Specimen Left Behind: mass digitization of natural history collections, *ZooKeys*, **209**, 87–92. doi: 10.3897/zookeys.209.3609.

26 Reed, S. (2010) Pushing DAISY, *Science*, **328**, 1628–9.

27 Parr, C. S., Guralnick, R., Cellinese, N. and Page, R. D. M. (2012) Evolutionary Informatics: unifying knowledge about the diversity of life, *Trends in Ecology & Evolution*, **27**, 94–103.

28 Smith, V. S. and Penev, L. (2011) Collaborative Electronic Infrastructures to Accelerate Taxonomic Research, *ZooKeys*, **150**, 1–3. doi: 10.3897/zookeys.150.2458.

29 Smith, V. S., Rycroft, S. D., Harman, K. T., Scott, B. and Roberts, D. (2009) Scratchpads: a data-publishing framework to build, share and manage information on the diversity of life, *BMC Bioinformatics*, **10** (Supp 1), S6.

30 Maddison, D. R. et al. (2012) Ramping up Biodiversity Discovery via Online Quantum Contributions, *Trends in Ecology and Evolution*, **27**, 72–7.

6

Coping with the data deluge

John Wood

ABSTRACT

The impact of the data deluge is affecting all disciplines – from the humanities to large-scale science. Making data openly available allows us to approach global challenges holistically. In many cases we need to assess human factors alongside the legal, medical and technology issues: for example, in the field of world energy demand. So there is a need for common standards for preservation and access in order to ensure interoperability. Yet the field is developing very fast, with many funders arguing that publicly funded research must be made publicly available. This does not simply mean that the data is dumped somewhere: it must be accessible to other researchers in an intelligible manner. Some large international projects are trying to solve these issues, and there is increasing evidence that governments have woken up to the issues. A key challenge will be for the researchers themselves. Projects in biodiversity, for example, require individual researchers to come together – physicists, space scientists and computer scientists working alongside biologists and environmental scientists. The management of such projects requires skills that few possess at present. Hence the need is urgent to look at how researchers are trained, how they manage such projects and the role of the data specialist. How will democracy work if data is publicly available in the future? This chapter seeks to open up these and many other issues that will affect society in fundamental ways. Informed debate is needed in order to ensure that the immense opportunities offered by the data deluge are not lost for future generations.

Introduction

> Upon this gifted age, in its dark hour,
> Falls from the sky a meteoric shower
> Of facts ... they lie unquestioned, uncombined.
> Wisdom enough to leech us of our ill
> Is daily spun; but there exists no loom
> To weave it into fabric ...[1]

We hear continuously the slogan 'data deluge'; but what does it mean, why has it suddenly become important and is it really going to affect the way in which research will be done and communicated to others in the future? Concerns about being overwhelmed by a flood of data have focused both on the impact of so-called e-science and its implications, and on the scale and complexity of many of the 'grand challenges' facing the research community and society at large. No longer are large data sets solely the domain of big science. Some of the key leaders in data-driven research are grappling with the anarchic world of individual databases that is now encountered in large international collaborations in the humanities and social sciences. Indeed the need to find commonly agreed international standards and protocols brings together researchers from all disciplines who realize that there is an urgent need to find a way forward that will allow different disciplines to share their data and to facilitate interoperability. While the initial focus has been on very large data sets, the integration of the myriads of smaller ones is also seen to be essential, and presents many more difficult challenges. A key question is whether any of this is realistic or whether we are just trying to create an edifice that is bound to fail.

A second set of concerns focuses on whether researchers, and especially those training the next generation, are able to think in a way that will enable cross-cutting, holistic research to be undertaken. For example, developments in linguistics research might affect how international agreements on climate mitigation are drafted. Whatever one's views, it is clear that there are great opportunities, but also significant risks; it is important, therefore, to avoid such dangers as introducing heavy-handed bureaucracy, discouraging outside-the-box thinking or allowing the best to become the enemy of the good. It is incumbent on all stakeholders to try to find workable solutions – which will vary according to the demands of a wide range of different contexts: national, regional, institutional and disciplinary. However, one thing is certain: research and innovation have to change if our world is to survive in the future, and much of this change will be related to the way in which data is handled and made accessible to all.

Opportunities and challenges

The first annual report of the European Research Area Board makes much of the role of e-science in tackling the major social, economic and technological challenges:

> We face mounting challenges: of global warming, scarce water, energy shortages and healthcare, to name a few. Their solution will require new ideas, discoveries, talents and innovations – the fruits of research. To achieve them, we must start by changing the way we do research.[2]

Similar points are made in the seminal book *The Fourth Paradigm*,[3] the publicity material for which states that:

> Increasingly, scientific breakthroughs will be powered by advanced computing capabilities that help researchers manipulate and explore massive datasets. The speed at which any given scientific discipline advances will depend on how well its researchers collaborate with one another, and with technologists, in areas of e-Science such as databases, workflow management, visualization, and cloud computing technologies.

And in the foreword of the same book Gordon Bell says that:

> In such scientific research, we are at a stage of development that is analogous to when the printing press was invented. Printing took a thousand years to develop and evolve into the many forms it takes today. Using computers to gain understanding from data created and stored in our electronic data stores will likely take decades – or less.

This all sounds very grand; but the European Commission, in a communication of 2012,[4] gives four more mundane reasons for the provision of 'fuller and wider access to scientific publications and data':

- accelerating innovation (faster to market = faster growth)
- fostering collaboration and avoiding duplication of effort (greater efficiency)
- building on previous research results (improved quality of results)
- involving citizens and society (improved transparency of the scientific process).

Many reports claim that wider access to, and better use of, data will accelerate scientific progress, improve the returns on investment in research and bring major economic advantages in the form of greater productivity, competitiveness and growth. A study undertaken in the UK estimated that the value of existing data in the UK was £25.1 billion in 2011 and that it would rise to £216 billion during the following five years.[5] A widely cited example of the value of data and information arises from the human genome project, which, as the European Commission notes,[4] is estimated to have cost various governments $3.8 billion, but which resulted in an economic impact of $796 billion and 310,000 jobs.[5] Whatever the basis for such estimates, it is clear that we are not talking about incremental changes.

So what do we mean by data? At one extreme it could be a measurement of one photon impacting on a sensor that can measure its energy and frequency via an electronic signal that can be stored in some form of electronic medium. At another extreme it could be a record of a historical event noted down in a diary, or a recording of a folk tale. The examples demonstrate that the recording of individual items of data without context is meaningless, and this poses a real problem for curators of data sets both large and small. How much background is it necessary to store in order to ensure that the data can be used by others? It is also necessary to distinguish between raw data and that which has been processed or amalgamated in some way, and between these and the contextual background – so-called metadata. A report in 2012 by the Royal Society stresses that data must be not only available but usable,[6] and emphasizes once again that the data may be used by many different people in different disciplines; and it stresses the importance of making data not only accessible but also intelligible, assessable and usable for a wide range of likely purposes. It uses these concepts to build the case for what it terms 'intelligent' openness. The report, which is addressed mainly to UK and mainstream science, distinguishes between data, information and knowledge. Data are defined as numbers, characters or images that designate an attribute of a phenomenon; data become information when they are combined together in ways that can reveal patterns in the phenomenon; and information yields knowledge when it supports non-trivial truth-claims about a phenomenon.

Putting it into practice: three European examples

How to handle data sets as they become linked to electronic publications, and how to determine what is worth keeping as we move to a more Open Access agenda are matters that are taxing minds across the globe. The number of meetings, summits and reports during the three years 2010 to 2012 – from the Royal Society[6] and the Centre for Economic and Business Research[5] in the UK; the Blue Ribbon Task Force in the USA;[7] the European Commission's High Level Expert Group on Scientific Data,[8] the E-infrastructure Reflection Group[9] and Knowledge Exchange[10] in Europe; and the Canadian Research Data Summit[11] – suggest that there can be little doubt that the issues are being taken seriously. This plethora of reports has come from all angles as governments, funders, academies and researchers have all begun to realize the importance of treating data responsibly, but at the same time in an economically sound and justifiable way. There now appears to be a firm resolve to try to create a co-ordinated (unified where appropriate) international approach to the complex area of data handling, sharing and all the ancillary issues. International efforts involving all the major countries of the world are now in train to create a consortium rather like the World Wide Web Consortium (W3C).

From the outside, these issues can look very dry. To put them in context it is worth looking at some of the pan-European projects that are at the forefront of this new approach to research.

The ELIXIR project (www.elixir-europe.org) brings together Europe's leading life science organizations to provide a pan-European infrastructure for biological information in order to manage and safeguard the massive amounts of data being generated every day by publicly funded research. It notes that:

> Life science research is becoming increasingly collaborative and complex, using several different technologies to understand organisms and diseases at the systems level. It is a significant challenge to integrate the wide variety of data coming out of life science experiments in meaningful, research-supportive ways.
>
> ELIXIR's vision for the future is to provide researchers in academia and industry with seamless access to biological information that will revolutionise discovery in the life sciences. This requires integrating data on many levels, from molecular biology to clinical practice.

The project's website points out that the rate of sequencing the human genome increased by 400 times in one decade from 2000, and that the rate is likely to increase by several orders of magnitude in the near future, resulting in exabytes of data being created each year. It also notes that the collection, curation, storage, archiving, integration and deployment of biomolecular data is an immense challenge that cannot be handled by a single organization or by one country alone, but requires international co-ordination.

The CLARIN project[12] seeks to establish an integrated and interoperable research infrastructure of language resources and technology and aims 'at lifting the current fragmentation, offering a stable, persistent, accessible and extendable infrastructure and therefore enabling e-Humanities':

> CLARIN will offer scholars the tools to allow computer-aided language processing, addressing the multiple roles language plays in the Humanities and Social Sciences. Language is not only a rich means of communication and a carrier of cultural content and knowledge, but also an important component of identity, an object of study.

The infrastructure that the project is creating will enable researchers to deposit and register language resources and tools and make them visible and accessible to others; to search for resources that are accessible; to create virtual collections of resources from different repositories; and to apply language technology tools to solve specific problems.

Finally, the LifeWatch project (www.lifewatch.eu) aims to drive forward the application of new information and communications technologies in studies of biodiversity and ecosystems. It also aims to promote new ways of collaboration, facilitating the sharing of data and providing specialized workflows and facilities for specific scientific communities:

> Users may benefit from integrated access to a variety of data, analytical and modelling tools as served by a variety of collaborating initiatives. Another service is offered with data and tools in selected workflows for specific scientific communities. In addition, LifeWatch will provide opportunities to construct personalized 'virtual labs', also allowing researchers to enter new data and to use specialized analytical tools.

These three examples show that the issues of data creation, provenance, storage, curation and long-term accessibility cut across all disciplines. Moreover, much of the fertile ground will be where these disciplines interact or share with other projects in related areas. CLARIN has joined several other projects to form the Coalition of Humanities and Arts Infrastructures and Networks (CHAIN), while LifeWatch is fostering interactions with ELIXIR and several other related activities.

These are exciting, fast-moving developments. In addition, many research funders are now insisting on a data management plan as part of any research proposal and that, with some restrictions, the resulting data be available to the public if the research has been publicly funded. This situation will impose requirements on both individual researchers and their institutions, for which few are yet ready.

One of the main implications of the new world of data is that it has the potential to change the way in which research is actually done. It allows large-scale and structural problems to be considered, and the way in which these are undertaken and managed becomes an important issue. CLARIN is a good example, where regional groups form and apply to join a consortium by agreeing certain criteria for the quality and availability of their data. However, the nerve centre for ensuring that standards are agreed and followed is managed on behalf of linguistic researchers worldwide by an electrical engineer who understands the computing and storage requirements necessary for their work. This use of a specialist in a completely different discipline to manage the data infrastructure is intriguing. For example, in LifeWatch, data will be captured in many ways and transmitted via satellite to the data analysis centre, which could be at CERN in Geneva. The data gatherer might be an amateur botanist armed with only a camera phone. If he sees a new or unexpected species he can transmit a photo to the data centre with the date, time, GPS co-ordinates and so on; this is added to the data coming from many other sources. These data can later be entered into large computer simulations to predict, for example, the effect of climate change on biodiversity and, subsequently, on food quality and health. In this way we can have an amateur observer linking via the European Space Agency to the European Centre for high-energy physics, which in turn has outsourced its data handling to a place where it can be stored and accessed most economically. Outputs from the simulations can then be used to inform government policy. From this one example, which is already happening, it can be seen how the whole ecosystem of research is changing.

Problems and questions

There are many technical issues to be resolved; but also more fundamental questions to be answered if the full potential of the data revolution is to be realized:

1   How will the data be preserved, as the media for storage changes rapidly? Is the 'cloud' the answer?
2   The need to guard against cyber-crime/terrorism is well known, and research data sets need to be protected as much as any other kinds of data. Hackers and those involved in industrial espionage have an interest in breaking in so as to create doubts about the reliability of data, especially where the original investigators have moved on. Should access be restricted? How can we reconcile this with the drive to make publicly funded data publicly available?
3   It has already been pointed out that data without context are useless. How much background is necessary if open access to data is to be realized to full effect?

It is generally agreed that data relating to individuals should not be available, yet it is becoming very difficult to anonymize data.

An underlying theme of all the recent work on these issues is the need for trust. *Riding the Wave* notes that:

Data-intensive science operates at a distance and in a distributed way, often among people who have never met, never spoken, and, sometimes, never communicated directly in any form whatsoever. They must share their results, opinions and data as if they were in the same room. But in truth, they have no real way of knowing for sure if, on the other end of the line, they will find a man or machine, collaborator or competitor, reliable partner or con-artist, careful archivist or data slob. And those problems concern merely the scientific community; what about when we add a wider population? How will we judge the reliability and authenticity of data that moves from a personal archive into a common scientific repository?[8]

Concerns about these issues pervade all the recent reports on data. *Riding the Wave*[8] recommends a form of global governance that is accepted by all who take part in data-intensive research. The National Science Foundation workshop on 'Changing the Conduct of Science in the Information Age'[13] discussed many of the technical and social issues. A basic requirement for better governance is that each researcher be identified and verified as a *bona fide* person who has signed up to the rules on sharing data. This is the so-called 'persistent identifier' label that allows anyone to check that someone is who they say they are and that they have made the necessary commitments. False identity is common in the world of social networking, and needs to be policed with particular care in the world of data networking. The Royal Society's report *Science as an Open Enterprise*[6] gives several examples of fraudulent science, which is set to increase as the amount of data increases and the means of checking become more problematic.

Scientific fraud is a downside of the increasing imperative to measure and assess research performance; in some countries the ability to earn an adequate salary is linked to the production of a certain number of publications in international journals (again, increasingly linked to primary data sets). It is argued in most reports that significant data sets should be cited in publications with due acknowledgement to their contributors and guardians. The recent recommendations of the European Commission on open access to data[14] state that credit should be given, in recruitment and career progression, to those researchers who participate in a culture of sharing results. Being easily identified and sharing results are not part of the common culture and practice for many researchers, so a carrot-and-stick approach may be needed.

Policy proposals

The *Riding the Wave* report[8] produced by the European Commission's High Level Expert Group on Scientific Data suggests a need for action under six main headings:

1   *To develop an international framework for a collaborative data infrastructure* to handle a diverse range of data, and which is flexible but reliable, secure yet open, local and global, and affordable yet high-performance, giving confidence to all who participate.
2   *To earmark additional funds for scientific e-infrastructure* to deal with data, and to recognize that such funding is required as a true cost of the research and not just as an add-on at the end of a project. Some of the base costs could be incorporated into local, regional or national infrastructures.
3   *To develop and use new ways to measure data value, and to reward those who contribute it*, recognizing that not all data is worth keeping.
4   *To train a new generation of data scientists, and broaden public understanding.* Researchers are generally uninterested in the long-term curation of their data and unaware of how this might be achieved. Conversely, most librarians lack in-depth experience in research methods and the multiple ways in which basic data are created. A new bridging discipline between these two groups, which is termed 'data scientist', is needed. The handling of data in this way should be instilled in students from secondary school level onwards.
5   *To create incentives for green technologies in the data infrastructure*, reducing the energy requirements for storing large amounts of data by developing new green technologies.
6   *To establish a high-level interministerial group on a global level to plan for data infrastructure*, and to create a common framework for the governance of data.

The recommendation or realization in the *Riding the Wave* report is that data itself becomes the basic infrastructure for scientific research. But how can this work in practice? Much of the data, such as personal data sets held on home computers or local hard discs, is transient. At the other extreme are those large data sets recording high-value and often one-off events. Between these two extremes lie groups of data that can range from subject-specific to project-wide. A data infrastructure has to be able to deal with all of these and present itself seamlessly to the subsequent user.

Future potential: training data creators, intermediaries and users

So how can we train researchers and information professionals, including librarians, to take advantage of this new and rapidly developing environment? It has already been stated that dealing with data and with the implications of making it generally available should start in school. By the time that students have started their research careers in a particular field, the reality of how and why this must be done needs to be second nature. But this may be difficult to achieve when so many academic supervisors are not aware of the potential of contributing to, and mining, a vast array of different data sets. Again we come back to the need for the new discipline of data science, with data scientists who can sit in a research group on equal terms with the domain-specialist researchers to advise as pro-active data archivists.

Is all this wishful thinking; and how can we provide appropriate incentives to encourage researchers to contribute positively to the data world? First, there is a growing tendency for funders to withhold payment of the last part of a grant unless they are assured that a robust data management plan is to be implemented. While this is good in theory, little thought has been given to how it might be policed in the long term. Second, it could become part of the final acceptance of a doctoral thesis that the data collected or derived is in a form that conforms to international standards and is accessible through an appropriate repository. Of course it would be much better if researchers could all begin to understand and internalize the value of contributing to and exchanging with international partners. All being well, this will come with time.

In the European Commission's *Recommendation on Access to and Preservation of Scientific Information*[14] there is a specific funding proposal to ensure that publicly funded data is publicly available, with due regard for privacy, trade secrets, national security etc.; that data sets are easily identifiable and can be linked to other data sets with metrics to evaluate their usefulness; and that researchers are rewarded positively by their institutions. A final point emerges from most reports: that there is a need for a trained and recognized cadre of data scientists who understand both the subject domain and the requirements of dealing with data, and who can act as intermediary between the researchers, librarians and other information specialists. The Royal Society's *Science as an Open Enterprise* report states that they must be mathematically adept and trained in the tools of data management. I would add to this the ability to interface across disciplines and to understand the real needs of both researchers and potential end-users. The report goes on to stress that the topic and tools are still at a very early stage of development, and that much research and development is needed if the full potential of the digital revolution is to be realized.

In this short chapter I have not been able to explore the most exciting area of 'Citizen Cyberscience'. At the 2012 2nd Citizen Cyberscience Summit (http://cybersciencesummit.org), held in London, dozens of exciting projects were presented in which digitized information had been accessed or contributed by several hundred thousand participants. Projects ranged widely: from the use of historical ships' log books not only to verify global weather simulations but also to follow the social history of ancestors and cultural changes; to deforestation; and to studies of how government policies around the world are affecting people's behaviour. Perhaps the best-known citizen science project is Galaxy Zoo, in which it is claimed that over 320,000 people participated in identifying over 120 million galaxy classifications, resulting in 25 peer group-reviewed publications. Many projects adopting similar approaches can be viewed by visiting the 'zooniverse' website (www.zooniverse.org).

More broadly, if data is freely available to all, what use will the citizen make of it all? There is real democratic power which could lead to greater public engagement in the research process, as well as with the results of research. There is a risk that if it were abused, say, by the popular press or by an extremist group, access to research data could result in serious damage to researchers and research. But if it is handled responsibly it could have positive influence on policy makers and show which policies are really effective.

Conclusion

In conclusion, the potential of data sets, both large and small, using modern digital technology, for research and innovation is at an embryonic stage. The potential to revolutionize how research of many different kinds is carried out and to facilitate the growth of 'citizen science' are as yet ill understood; but the potential, if properly harnessed, is immense.

References

1 Millay, E. St Vincent (1939) Sonnet X. In: *Huntsman What Quarry?*, Harper.
2 European Research Area Board (2009) *Preparing Europe for a New Renaissance: a strategic view of the European Research Area*, European Commission.
3 Hey, T., Tansley, S. and Tolle K (eds) (2009) *The Fourth Paradigm*, Microsoft Research.
4 European Commission (2012) *Towards Better Access to Scientific Information: boosting the benefits of public investments in research*.
5 Centre for Economic and Business Research (2012) *Data Equity: unlocking the value of big data*, SAS.
6 Royal Society (2012) *Science as an Open Enterprise*.
7 Blue Ribbon Task Force on Sustainable Digital Preservation and Access (2010) *Sustainable Economics for a Digital Planet – Ensuring Long-term Access to Digital Information*.
8 High Level Expert Group on Scientific Data (2010) *Riding the Wave – How Europe Can Gain from the Rising Tide of Scientific Data*, European Commission.
9 e-Infrastructure Reflection Group (2012) *e-IRG 'Blue Paper' on Data Management*.
10 Knowledge Exchange (2011) *A Surfboard for Riding the Wave: towards a four country action programme on research data*.
11 Research Data Strategy Working Group (2011) *Mapping the Data Landscape: Report of the 2011 Canadian Research Data Summit*.
12 www.clarin.eu/external/index.php?page=about-clarin.
13 National Science Foundation (2011) *Changing the Conduct of Science in an Information Age: summary report of workshop held on November 12, 2010*, NSF.
14 European Commission (2012) *Recommendation on Access to and Preservation of Scientific Information*, European Commission, C(2012) 4890 final.

7

Social media and scholarly communications: the more they change, the more they stay the same?

Ellen Collins

ABSTRACT

Social media have been hailed as a significant opportunity for scholarly communications, offering researchers new and effective ways to discover and share knowledge. Tools such as blogs, wikis, Twitter and Facebook, as well as their underpinning principles such as crowdsourcing and the value of enhanced or networked data, have all been explored to varying extents by academics, librarians and publishers in their attempts to improve the efficiency of scholarly communications and to reach new or wider audiences. This chapter examines such use of social media and suggests that all of these groups use social media only where it mimics or reinforces their existing behaviours. For the most part, they adopt those elements of social media that make tasks easier or more efficient, but reshape tools or the way in which they are used in order to avoid challenging traditional cornerstones of scholarly communications, such as journal articles and peer review.

Introduction

Facebook was founded in 2004: by January 2009 it had 175 million active users; and by December 2011 it had 845 million – around 12% of the world's population.[1] Twitter was launched in July 2006 and signed up its 100 millionth active user in September 2011.[2] In September 2010, the five billionth photograph was added to Flickr's searchable database;[3] the Tate group of four art galleries has a collection of just 65,000 works of art.[4]

These statistics show how social media have rapidly become a routine part of many people's personal and professional lives. This chapter explores how these new tools, and the behaviours that underpin their use, are being adopted within scholarly communications, and whether they are changing the way in which researchers and others share information and knowledge.

The social media landscape

Social media tools and technologies build upon the principles and practices of Web 2.0. These stress the move from static, proprietary systems to applications which 'get better the more people use them'.[5] Web 2.0 focuses on tools which treat the user as a co-developer and on business models which seek to generate revenue not from sales of a product but from services or enhanced data. Crucially, content generated by the user becomes the source of the providing company's value: either through network effects, as with Facebook, or by adding value to widely available existing data sets, as with the rating and recommender services which overlay standard bibliographic data on Amazon.

Kaplan and Haenlein[6] classify social media tools on two scales. The first describes the extent to which the tool allows participants to communicate with each other, without intermediation and in real time: tools on this spectrum might range from blogs, which are at the low end of the scale, to virtual social worlds such as Second Life, where anybody can talk to anybody else in real time. The second scale describes the amount of personal information that users can, or must, disclose: tools on this scale might range from YouTube, where users do not have to share personal information in order to get value from the service, to Facebook, the value of which depends upon the personal information shared by users.

Social media share many aims in common with scholarly communications. This is particularly apparent if we take the broad definition of scholarly communications offered by Thorin,[7] encompassing not just the process of publication and discovery of formal research findings in journals, conferences and books, but also the more informal ways in which researchers communicate with each other throughout the research process, and how they engage with wider audiences.

At both the formal and informal ends of the scale, the scholarly communications system has shown itself able to adapt to new technologies and ways of working. The internet has brought increases in the availability and usage of journal articles.[8–10] It has also expanded the ways in which researchers can communicate with each other informally through, for example, e-mail listservs such as the UK's JISCMail service, which runs thousands of lists with over a million members in total.[11]

But it is not clear that these new technologies have brought a qualitative change in how researchers communicate and share information. Nicholas et al.[12] suggest that 'power browsing', although made easier by online formats, did not originate with them, while others have pointed to how most electronic publications present simply a PDF reproduction of print formats.[13] Researchers' attitudes have not fully kept up with new technologies, and online-only publications are still rated less highly than print versions in many disciplines.[13–15] Since social media comprise both a set of tools and an underlying philosophy about how they should be used to facilitate information exchange, we must consider not just whether the tools are adopted, but also whether they have affected the underpinning principles of scholarly communication.

Recent studies have begun to explore how researchers interact with social media. Taken together, they suggest some observable trends in researchers' uptake of these new tools. Most researchers are, at best, infrequent users of social media: one study found that just 13% of researchers used Web 2.0 tools at least once a week.[14] One important reason for low uptake, found across several studies, is the time that it takes to learn how to use these new tools, and their fragmented and specialized nature.[14, 16, 17]

Typically – confounding expectations about the 'Google generation' – young researchers are less likely to experiment with these tools than are their older and more senior colleagues.[12, 14, 17] This may be because younger scholars must focus on building their reputations by producing publications and other outputs that fit with established academic conventions. Older researchers with established reputations can afford to experiment with new formats, particularly when such experimentation might expose their work to a wider audience.[14]

The influence of discipline on researchers' information behaviour is well known.[18] But with social media there seems to be a linkage between uptake and perceived support from colleagues, peers and institutional services.[14, 19] Whether greater use follows better support, or whether researchers who are already using tools see support where others would not, there is an important relationship here.

Perhaps in recognition of this relationship, development teams in some universities are providing guidance and information for researchers who are interested in engaging with social media but unsure about where to begin.[20] Many libraries are attempting to support researchers in their use of new technologies[21] and also to use social media themselves in order to engage with their users, although success in this area can be mixed and they do not always have clear aims in their engagement with social media.[22–3]

Many publishers are also engaging with the possibilities offered by social media. In many cases, this is driven by a desire to consolidate their brand's online presence by connecting informal discussions on Twitter or blogs to original articles;[14] but some publishers have also begun to experiment with direct engagement with their authors and readers. Nature Publishing Group, for example, has developed a number of tools which, while targeted at academic researchers, mimic generic social media services such as blogging, commenting, networks and tagging or bookmarking.[24]

The rest of this chapter will consider how the use of social media has affected three key areas of scholarly communications: first, information management within projects – how researchers communicate with their colleagues and a wider disciplinary community as they conduct their research; second, formal scholarly publication – how researchers register, quality assure, disseminate and discover online content; and third, wider scholarly communication – how researchers engage with current affairs, news and less formal communication of research results.

Information management in projects

Social media aim to make it easier to share information in an open way. They could thus be a natural home for the kinds of informal communications that occur during the research process itself – the conversations between researchers and others as they establish and scope a research project and collect and share initial findings. Some researchers have begun to adopt social media for these purposes, sometimes using tools specifically designed for academics, but more commonly adopting and adapting generic services designed for a wider audience.[12]

Collaboration in research is increasingly important: between departments and institutions, and between academia and industry.[25–6]

Managing information in such collaborations can be complex, and some researchers use social media to organize the different kinds of communication that keep research projects moving. Wikis and open lab notebooks provide new ways for researchers to communicate with their immediate colleagues;[27-8] but usage varies by discipline, and is also strongly influenced by the behaviour and attitudes of other researchers in the team. For most researchers, social media are not a primary tool for project administration.[26]

Researchers also use social media to seek help in answering specific, often methodological, questions. They might, like the researcher who asked about a biomedical research technique on Facebook,[20] seek help from their friends and colleagues; or they might draw on the wider research community through tools such as StackExchange (http://stackexchange.com/), StackOverflow (http://stackoverflow.com/) and MathOverflow (http://mathoverflow.net/), where researchers post and answer precise and specialized questions. These tools use the Web 2.0 'wisdom of crowds' techniques as a means of quality control, allowing users to recommend good questions or answers and (once they have established their credibility) to remove poor ones. Use of these tools is strongest in disciplines – such as physics, mathematics, economics and linguistics – where researchers commonly work together with an extended network of peers. They have not made significant inroads into other disciplines, such as history.[16, 25, 28]

Crowdsourcing has begun to make an impact at other stages of the research process, too. The Zooniverse (https://www.zooniverse.org/) group of projects generates data based upon the analysis by thousands of 'citizen scientists' of images of galaxies, historic ships' logs, ancient papyri and other primary sources not suitable for machine analysis. Each data point is classified by tens, sometimes hundreds, of web users, giving researchers a strong consensus and assurance as to the quality of the work, while identifying contested units which must be examined by more experienced researchers.[28] The entire enterprise relies upon the principle that Web 2.0 tools get better as more people use them.[5]

Zooniverse and StackExchange reflect the open principles of Web 2.0: anybody is free to contribute to the scientific process and the value of their contribution is recognized and signalled. Some Zooniverse citizen scientists have been added as co-authors of papers to which they have made valuable contributions. Researchers who operate in an environment where some of their communications must remain private, however, use social media tools in a much more restricted way. For example, in order to protect future publication opportunities, 'people don't put their notebooks on a public blog or wiki for people to read until they've published the paper'.[27] Sometimes social media tools are set up to 'require a login just so that people within the project feel free to write everything down warts and all in progress'.[27]

Formal publication

Researchers must publish their work – mainly in books and scholarly journals – in order to build their academic careers; and researchers do not regard social media as a wholesale replacement for those channels.[16, 25, 28] Researchers in some disciplines – philosophy, for example – publish early drafts of their work using social media tools such as blogs, seeking comments from their peers. But such behaviour continues the tradition of circulating working papers and pre-prints, rather than being a new behaviour stimulated by social media. The early drafts are not considered a 'publication' of the same standing as a journal article.[25, 29]

One reason why researchers cling tightly to established communication mechanisms is the quality-assurance systems provided by publishers. The reputations of presses and journals are built over many years, and new entrants to the market must be able to provide similar and recognizable indicators of quality.[30] Many critiques of social media are based upon a perceived lack of effective quality assurance, and a mistrust of platforms which have not built academic credibility. Wikipedia comes in for particular opprobrium from some researchers because of its lack of formal peer-review mechanisms; others suggest that it is most useful as a place to find references to the peer-reviewed literature, rather than as a source in itself.[14, 25]

Despite numerous outreach efforts, researchers have been reluctant to help to improve the quality of Wikipedia articles in their subject area.[31–2] In order to increase academic contributions, and thus its credibility, Wikipedia is considering a proposal for a peer-reviewed Open Access journal: academics would write a Wikipedia-style article which would then be submitted for blind peer review and published in the journal. The proposers believe that offering academics a traditional and familiar reward structure will encourage them to contribute.[33] In this instance, far from adapting their practices to fit with the new form of communication, researchers are seeking to force the social media platform to change its behaviour so as to meet their needs.

Wikipedia's collaborative, anonymous editing process is not recognized by researchers as a trustworthy source of peer review: high-profile incidents of 'gaming', such as Orlando Figes' behaviour on Amazon reviews, may have helped to reinforce this view.[34] Publishers' experiments with crowd-sourced quality assurance through, for example, user comments, have not always been successful. *Nature* struggled to convince both its editors and its readers of the value of reader comments on journal articles: both were concerned about protecting their brand – either as publishers or as researchers – within a mechanism that is essentially informal and even throwaway. *BMJ* has had more success in encouraging comments below its articles; it may help that such comments are considered an extension of 'letters to the editor' and assigned a digital object identifier which can be cited.[24] *PLoS One* uses traditional peer review to ensure the academic rigour of articles before they are published, reserving social media (along with other measures of impact) to determine the significance of content post-publication.[14] Once again, social media must adapt to traditional scholarly mores in order to be accepted.

Once research is published, some researchers use social media to promote, discover and organize it. Twitter and blogs become sources of information about new, interesting publications; so do purpose-built tools such as academia.edu (http://academia.edu/), which allows researchers to post their papers so that other researchers can find and follow them. This may be seen as an extension of existing information practices, where researchers use recommendations from their colleagues as a way to find content in books and journals.[35] Researchers also use social media to organize the research that they read, and this is perhaps the area where purpose-built tools have had the most cross-disciplinary success. Services such as Mendeley (www.mendeley.com/) and Zotero (www.zotero.org) present a combination of traditional reference management functionalities, overlaid with tools such as social tagging, groups and social networks. Again, though, use of these services need not be as open as Web 2.0 principles might suggest. Although Mendeley is available on a web platform, it is designed to be downloaded to local devices, thereby failing

O'Reilly's definition of Web 2.0 as operating on platforms, rather than applications.[36] Furthermore, Mendeley makes it easy for researchers to behave in a 'closed' way, limiting access to their list of publications and annotations to invited groups of co-investigators, or keeping them entirely private. This sets such services apart from social networks such as Facebook, where there is little or no value in keeping content entirely to oneself.

Wider communications

Social media are beginning to change how researchers engage with the wider information world that they inhabit. Many researchers use blogs, Twitter and other services to keep up to date on wider developments in academia – political campaigns, gossip or job and funding opportunities.[14, 28] Publishers and librarians are beginning to recognize this, and to use social media themselves in order to engage more effectively with the research communities that they wish to serve.

Among these actors, again, we see a distinction between the services offered and the engagement with underlying social media philosophies. For example, many librarians have developed Facebook pages, believing that this offers them a good way to communicate with researchers – although 54% believe that there is no academic value to Facebook.[37] However, they also recognize that many users – especially undergraduates – may not want to use Facebook to communicate with teachers or librarians.[23] Other studies have shown that most librarians undertake 0–20 minutes of maintenance on their Facebook pages each week – less than necessary if they were fully interacting with their users to co-develop useful services.[37] This is not to say that the philosophy of social media is not evident anywhere among libraries: Library 2.0, as outlined by Casey and Savastinuk,[38] focuses upon what users want, and concentrating on a process of constant change and evaluation to ensure that services deliver this. However, technology is only a very small part of this vision, and the relationship between libraries' use of social media tools and their adoption of social media philosophy is thus rather distant.

Publishers are in a similar situation. Many use Twitter feeds to announce new articles, and blogs to provide a more 'newsy' take on issues within specific fields. But these tend to be a more informal way for journals or publishers to communicate with their readers, rather than a two-way conversation. It is rare to see the active engagement with researchers shown by Nature Publishing Group via its Nature Networks and, previously, Nature Blogs services. Nature Networks offers researchers a range of services, including discussion forums and a platform for blogging, and is constantly developed by the Nature team through interaction with users. Nature Blogs used to offer access to a 'white list' of around a thousand science bloggers who were syndicated by Nature; it has now become a platform primarily for Nature staff to communicate with readers (similar to the services offered by, for example, *BMJ*), with external bloggers moved to Nature Networks. This move perhaps reflects a need to retain control over the core Nature brand. Many publishers engaging in social media have a similar concern.[24]

Conclusions

Social media are beginning to make their mark on scholarly communications, but not yet in a sustained or systematic way. Researchers are adopting some social media tools, where they see an advantage in doing so, and other actors in the scholarly communications system are responding by providing some social media functionality as part of their services. Overall, though, as Proctor et al.[14] conclude, there is no evidence of a sustained adoption of social media that is altering the way in which researchers do their work.

The most visible social media activity in the scholarly communications sphere tends to cluster around the lower ends of both the interactivity and disclosure dimensions set out in the introduction to this chapter. Social media are used primarily for information exchange, using technologies such as wikis or blogs which do not rely upon real-time communication. It may be that researchers are most comfortable where their communications are mediated or moderated – which may explain some of the success of BMJ comments, which are treated as original publications and edited in the same way as letters to the editor. Researchers may also be reluctant to reveal too much personal or professional information to a wide and unvetted audience: this is why students are reluctant to become 'friends' with their library on Facebook, and why project wikis tend to remain closed to those outside the research process.

Adoption of the philosophies that underlie social media has been mixed, with researchers considering whether those philosophies are appropriate to a particular purpose within academia. Take, for example, the philosophy of the wisdom of crowds. Adopting this philosophy by seeking comments on journal articles has not been especially successful as a means of quality assurance. Perhaps this is right: many research outputs are so highly specialized that reviewing them is not the same as rating a popular bestseller on Amazon, where any reader's opinion might be considered valid. But the philosophy has had more success when applied to data collection, as with the Zooniverse group of projects. Here, crowd wisdom allows real-time validation of results, ensuring that the mistakes of one or two amateur researchers do not affect overall data collection and, as a result, significantly advancing the ability of professional academics to collect and process data. The addition of citizen scientists as authors of published papers also suggests that social media philosophies have begun to change perceptions of who a researcher actually is – a fundamental change in the research landscape.

Researchers tend to adopt social media in ways that mimic, and perhaps reinforce, their existing priorities and principles. The uptake of social media tools for posting pre-prints and asking and answering methodological questions is most prominent in those disciplines which already had a tradition of working in extended collaborations and of sharing draft papers. There is no evidence of a widespread shift towards using social media as an alternative way of formally publishing research findings. Usage seems to focus upon discovery of information – extending the academic networks that have always been an important part of information discovery – or communicating about events in the wider research environment.

Overall, then, social media are not yet shifting the nature of scholarly communications. They are extending the reach and ease of traditional scholarly functions such as finding, sharing and organizing information; but they have failed to break through the long-standing academic attachment to conventions including formal journal articles and blind pre-publication peer review. While they have had a significant impact in certain areas, such as the collection of non-machine-readable data, these areas are limited and discipline specific. Of course, these are early days for social media tools: they have become widely used only in the last six or seven years. Academic conventions have been built up over hundreds of years: it is not realistic to expect them to alter overnight in the face of new technologies which change the ways in which people can communicate. Only time will tell whether the kinds of novel usage outlined in this chapter represent a new road for scholarly communications, or an academic cul-de-sac.

References

1 Facebook, *Factsheet*,
   http://newsroom.fb.com/content/default.aspx?NewsAreaId=22.
2 McMillan, G. (2011) Twitter Reveals Active User Number, How Many Actually Say Something, *Time Techland*, (9 September),
   http://techland.time.com/2011/09/09/twitter-reveals-active-user-number-how-many-actually-say-something/.
3 Sutter, J. (2010) 5 Billionth Photo Uploaded to Flickr, *CNN Tech*, (20 September), http://articles.cnn.com/2010-09-20/tech/flickr.5.billion_1_photo-sharing-site-flickr-facebook?_s=PM:TECH).
4 Tate, *About Us*, www.tate-images.com/TheCompany.asp.
5 O'Reilly, T. (2006) Web 2.0 Compact Definition: trying again, *O'Reilly Media*, (10 December), http://radar.oreilly.com/2006/12/web-20-compact-definition-tryi.html.
6 Kaplan, A. M. and Haenlein, M. (2010) Users of the World, Unite! The challenges and opportunities of social media, *Business Horizons*, **53**, 59–68.
7 Thorin, S. E. (2006) Global Changes in Scholarly Communication. In: Hsianghoo, S. C., Poon, P. W. T. and McNaught, C. (eds) *eLearning and Digital Publishing*, Springer.
8 Cox, J. and Cox, L. (2010) *E-only Scholarly Journals: overcoming the barriers*, Research Information Network.
9 Research Information Network (2010) *Trends in the Finances of UK Higher Education Libraries: 1999–2009*, Research Information Network.
10 Nicholas, D., Rowlands, I., Huntington, P., Clark, D. and Jamali, H. (2009) *E-journals: their use, value and impact*, Research Information Network.
11 JISC, *JISCMail*, www.jisc.ac.uk/whatwedo/services/jiscmail.aspx.
12 Nicholas, D., Rowlands, I. and Wamae, D. (2010) Are Social Media Impacting on Research? In Charleston Information Group, *XXX Annual Charleston Conference, 4–6 November, Charleston, NC*, www.ucl.ac.uk/infostudies/research/ciber/Charleston-2010.pdf, UCL, London.

13 Adema, J. and Rutten, P. (2010) *Digital Monographs in the Humanities and Social Sciences: report on user needs*, OAPEN.

14 Proctor, R., Williams, R. and Stewart, J. (2010) *If You Build It, Will They Come? How researchers perceive and use Web 2.0*, Research Information Network,

15 Steele, C. (2008) Scholarly Monograph Publishing in the 21st Century: the future more than ever should be an open book, *Journal of Electronic Publishing*, **11** (2), http://quod.lib.umich.edu/j/jep/ 3336451.0011.201?rgn=main;view=fulltext.

16 Williams, R., Pryor, G., Bruce, A., Macdonald, S. and Marsden, W. (2009) *Patterns of Information Use and Exchange: case studies of researchers in the life sciences*, Research Information Network.

17 Carpenter, J., Wetheridge, L., Smith, N., Goodman, M. and Struijvé, O. (2010) *Researchers of Tomorrow: annual report 2009–2010*, Education for Change.

18 Harley, D., Krzys Acord, S., Earl-Novell, S., Lawrence, S. and Judson King, C. (2010) *Assessing the Future Landscape of Scholarly Communication: an exploration of faculty values and needs in seven disciplines*, Center for Studies in Higher Education (CSHE), University of California.

19 Carpenter, J., Tanner, S., Smith, N. and Goodman, M. (2011) *Researchers of Tomorrow: annual report 2010–2011*, Education for Change.

20 Hooley, T., Cann, A. and Dimitriou, K. (2011) *Social Media: a guide for researchers*, Research Information Network.

21 Stone, G. and Collins, E. (2011) 25 Research Things @ Huddersfield: engaging researchers with social media, *ALISS Quarterly*, **7** (1), 11–15.

22 Jacobson, T. (2011) Facebook as a Library Tool: perceived vs. actual use, *College & Research Libraries*, **72** (1), 79–90.

23 Breeding, M. (2007) Librarians Face Online Social Networks, *Computers in Libraries*, (September), www.librarytechnology.org/ltg-displaytext.pl?RC=12735.

24 Stewart, J., Procter, R., Poschen, M. and Williams, R. (forthcoming) Academic Publishers as Innovation Intermediaries in the Development of Web 2.0 Services for Scholarly Communication, *New Media and Society*. Prepublished December 5, 2012 as doi:10.1177/1461444812464470.

25 Bulger, M., Meyer, E., de la Flor, G., Terras, M., Wyatt, S., Jirotka, M., Eccles, C. and Madsen, C. (2011) *Reinventing Research? Information practices in the humanities*, Research Information Network.

26 Jordan, E., Hunter, A., Seale, B., Thomas, A. and Levitt, R. (2011)

Information Handling in Collaborative Research: an exploration of five case studies, Research Information Network.

27 RIN/NESTA (2010) *Open to All? Case studies of openness in research*, Research Information Network.

28 Meyer, E., Bulger, M., Kyriakidou-Zacharoudiou, A., Power, L., Williams, P., Venters, W., Terras, M. and Wyatt, S. (2011) *Collaborative Yet Independent: information practices in the physical sciences,* Research Information Network.

29 Collins, E., Bulger, M. and Meyer, E. (2012) Discipline matters: technology use in the humanities, *Arts and Humanities in Higher Education*, **11** (2), 76–92.

30 Willinsky, J. (2009) Towards the Design of an Open Monograph Press, *Journal of Electronic Publishing*, **12** (1), http://quod.lib.umich.edu/j/jep/3336451.0012.103/—toward-the-design-of-an-open-monograph-press?rgn=main;view=fulltext;q1=willinsky.

31 Corbyn, Z. (2011) Wikipedia Wants More Contributions from Academic, *Guardian*, (29 March). www.guardian.co.uk/education/2011/mar/29/wikipedia-survey-academic-contributions

32 Banaji, M. (2011) Harnessing the Power of Wikipedia for Scientific Psychology: a call to action, *APS Observer*, (11 February), www.psychologicalscience.org/index.php/publications/observer/2011/february-11/harnessing-the-power-of-wikipedia-for-scientific-psychology-a-call-to-action.html.

33 Wikimedia Strategic Planning. *Proposal: journal (a peer-review journal to allow/encourage academics to write Wikipedia articles)*, http://strategy.wikimedia.org/wiki/Proposal:Journal_%28A_peer-review_journal_to_allow/encourage_academics_to_write_Wikipedia_articles%29.

34 Lea, R. and Taylor, M. (2010) Historian Orlando Figes Admits Posting Amazon Reviews that Trashed Rivals, *Guardian*, (23 April), www.guardian.co.uk/books/2010/apr/23/historian-orlando-figes-amazon-reviews-rivals.

35 Tenopir, C., Volentine, R. and King, D. W. (2012) *UK Scholarly Reading and the Value of Library Resources: summary results of the study conducted spring 2011,* JISC Collections, www.jisc-collections.ac.uk/Documents/Reports/UK%20Scholarly%20Reading%20and%20the%20Value%20of%20Library%20Resources%20Final%20Report.pdf.

36 O'Reilly, T. (2005) What Is Web 2.0? *O'Reilly.com*, (30 September), http://oreilly.com/web2/archive/what-is-web-20.html.

37 Hendrix, D., Chiarella, D., Hasman, L., Murphy, S. and Zafron, M. (2009)

Use of Facebook in Academic Health Sciences Libraries, *Journal of the Medical Library Association*, **97** (1), 44–7.
38 Casey, M. and Savastinuk, L. (2007) We Know What Library 2.0 Is and Is Not, *LibraryCrunch*, (31 October), www.librarycrunch.com/2007/10/we_know_what_library_20_is_and.html.

8

The changing role of the publisher in the scholarly communications process

Richard Bennett

ABSTRACT

The advent of digital communication has created challenges for publishers of scholarly materials; it has threatened to revolutionize the process of scholarly communication and change the fundamentals of the publishing process forever. But has it? This chapter investigates to what extent scholarly publishing has been affected by the transition to digital communication, what opportunities have been created and how the transition is shaping the future of the industry. It breaks down the publishing process into three stages – input, processing and output – to analyse how much each of these areas has been affected and if some areas of the publishing process have been affected more than others. It analyses the changing business models in the scholarly journals market and looks at the effect that the introduction of Open Access (OA) publishing has had on both the subscription business model and the way that the communication of research is being financed. It finds that scholarly publishers have undergone a huge transition over the last 20 years, moving from a slow, print-based model to purely digital delivery in many cases; but for all that change, the process of scholarly publishing (peer review, editorial review and the structure of a scientific paper) has changed very little. What has changed is the way that users are using and accessing the information, and the business models that have now developed for digital media, such as the Big Deal and Gold OA. Many scholarly publishers are still in the middle of a transition to true digital publishing and the mechanisms involved in scholarly communication have yet to take full advantage of many of the technologies available today, and so this industry will have to continue to adapt and change to meet the needs of the next generation of researchers.

Introduction

The publishing side of the scholarly communication process has developed over hundreds of years, with many crediting the invention of the Gutenberg printing press in around 1440 as the starting-point. This invention led to the mechanization of book making and the start of mass reproduction of intellectual works, which over time grew into the modern publishing industry. Many of the scientific publishers still trading today can trace their roots back many centuries and have developed alongside the growth of science as an area of interest and research, playing a role in the communication of its discoveries. In all that time the process itself has not altered greatly, and the structure of the physical book today is very similar to that of the books that first came off Gutenberg's press. Even scientific journals can trace their roots back to 1665, with the first issue of *Journal des Sçavans*, and although it wasn't until the second half of the 18th century that the scientific journal really took off, this puts into perspective the speed of the change that has occurred with the advent of digital publishing.

The first refereed scientific journal to be published in electronic form appeared in 1987, and the word 'e-journal', now so commonly used, was coined only in 1991, with the launch of *EJournal*, which was, incidentally, an electronic journal concerned with the implications of electronic networks and texts. In the 25 years or so that have passed since 1987, words and phrases such as digitization, electronic supplementary data, social media, PDF, XML, ePub, APIs and discovery layers have become commonplace, and publishers have had to respond rapidly to each wave of technological development. It is somewhat strange, therefore, to realize that the actual content, journal articles and book chapters, the very building blocks of scholarly communication, have not significantly changed in structure, while the discovery, distribution and management of that content has changed beyond recognition.

To analyse fully the effect that digitization has had on the role of the publisher in the scholarly communication process, the publishing process is broken down in this chapter into three stages:

- *Input:* Publishers must have content in order to be able to publish. This section will focus on the way in which the move to digital is changing the manner in which publishers interact with authors and editors. It will also look at how some of the long-held formats of publishing are being adapted and altered to fit into a digital environment.

■ *Processing:* Once accepted, papers and manuscripts have to be processed. The content has to be tagged, metadata has to be created and multiple output formats need to be produced.

■ *Output:* The distribution and accessibility of content has been completely changed by the digitization revolution; innovations in business models, such as the 'Big Deal' and the growth of Open Access (OA), are changing revenue and funding streams and creating challenges and opportunities for publishers. Developments in social media and search engine technology have changed the way that publishers interact with their readers; and the main customer base is undergoing its own major structural change process.

The input process

Delivering content digitally has not changed the fundamental nature of the author/publisher relationship in the STM sector – yet. Authors still create manuscripts and convey them to publishers for three basic purposes: copy-editing and typesetting; marketing; and monetization via sales. While some authors talk about posting their work on the internet and letting their colleagues have unfettered access, the percentage of authors who actually do this is very small. Scientists, who are daily overwhelmed by the amount of literature available to them, still see a value in working with STM publishers to launch their work in a manner that authenticates it and makes it easily findable within recognizable collections.

Publishing has become a lot faster, thanks entirely to digital workflows and digital distribution. In the early 1990s it took 16 weeks to produce a journal issue (from receiving the final manuscripts from the editorial office to printing). Today the same articles are published and available in 21 days or less. Journals can publish fully copy edited, typeset and proofread final copy in two to three weeks (as compared with two to three months in the not-so-distant past).

Publishers are using tools such as Twitter and Facebook to interact with both their author and reader communities, but most processes, particularly peer review, have not changed much at all. Reviewers may receive a manuscript immediately, but they still need time to read it, check details and ponder their conclusions before communicating their opinion to the editorial board. Book publishing is faster … once the complete manuscript is in hand. Simple, text-only books can be produced in two to three months (as compared to up to 12 months in the past). Often the rate-limiting step is delivery of the final chapter, which is rarely the 'final' chapter in the sequence. To get around the problem of being held hostage by the 'delinquent' author, there is a move by publishers towards 'online first chapter' publishing for books, whereby chapters are published online as they are completed and are later compiled into their final sequence.

Even the last step of compilation into a book is, in the digital world, becoming a matter of tradition rather than necessity, as online readers do not exhibit a reading pattern that is consistent with such a need. The average number of chapters used within the e-publisher Springerlink per user/per session is 1.2, which illustrates that the sequential nature of a book's construction is less relevant than the information provided by an individual chapter. This argument is best illustrated by the development of the structure of e-only journals, where 'online first' publishing (where articles are published online before being collated into an issue) is beginning to disappear and is being replaced by 'article-wise' publishing, with no journal issues at all. Without the print component, the need for articles to be collated into issues is diminished, allowing for the content to be aggregated and presented in different ways, such as by common subject content rather than by date of publication.

Another development is looking at a 'database' approach to book publishing. Rather than creating a collection of 'tables of contents', a matrix of content is built around a unifying theme – stem cells, for example. Micro-experts from around the world are invited to submit chapters on a wide variety of topics, and as each chapter is completed it is published 'online first'. When a critical mass of material is available, it is assembled into a volume and released. This process was developed to match the 'chapter-wise' downloading of e-book content and is an example of how usage data is changing the way in which scholarly information is being captured and presented.

Some content types have moved faster in their use of digital publishing tools than have others, mostly because of the need to solve a specific problem. One example of this is large reference works, which are often out of date by the time that they are published in print because of the extremely long timeline needed for their development. A solution to this has been the development of 'live' reference works that follow the example of Wikipedia and allow the original authors to update the digital version of their reference entry with up-to-the minute information. The difference from Wikipedia is that in the scholarly sphere there needs to be a review process, and so these new entries go through peer review before they appear as final entries. As we are still in a multi-format (both print and electronic) phase of content use, these updated reference works can be released as new print editions at a later date; however, it is not too far-fetched to assume that the print edition might be phased out over time.

Open Access

There have been various publisher reactions to OA: from denial to obstruction, to acceptance and promotion. It is fair to say that this is one of the most dramatic shifts in the business of scholarly publishing that we have seen. (As of September 2012 there were 8098 peer-reviewed OA journals listed in the Directory of Open Access Journals [DOAJ].) It has led to changes in funding; mandates to deposit publications in open access repositories (both funded and non-funded) from academic institutions and funding bodies; and the development of entirely new publishers and publishing programmes. From the publisher's perspective, disruptive change can be either a threat or an opportunity, and scholarly publishers generally started by dividing between those resistant to OA and those who embraced it as a new and different model of publishing. Nowadays there is a general acceptance of OA by the majority of publishers and most have instituted some sort of OA model in their existing journal programmes.

In effect, though, the OA process is essentially the same as the traditional publishing process, with the submission of a paper, peer review and dissemination of the final, approved article. The main difference is that the costs of publishing are borne by the author rather than the publisher, and the final article is freely accessible to all. OA and subscription business models tend to sit side by side in traditional publishing houses and many of the publishing processes can be merged, so that publishers can easily produce both subscription articles and OA articles alongside one another. For a scholarly publisher, author-paid OA

(Gold OA) can take two routes: pure OA journals, or OA articles published within traditional subscription journals (the so-called Hybrid OA model). Each of these options has been relatively successful, and the growth rates of OA in the market are significant. Overall, however, OA still represents a relatively small percentage of the scholarly articles published annually and still tends to be focused in a few areas of research, such as biomedicine and life sciences.

OA will continue to grow and will push changes in the scholarly publishing environment. One of the main advantages of pure OA journals is that they lower the barrier to entry into the journal market and make it possible to focus on very niche or new areas of research that may not have been financially viable in a traditional subscription model. Conversely, there is also a trend towards multi-disciplinary pure OA journals, such as *PLoS One*, which covers all areas of primary research.

The process of digital publishing

The traditional process of screening, editing and reviewing papers and manuscripts has not changed with the advent of digital publishing, although communication between the main parties is now done digitally and the entire process is managed by computer systems. The main changes have centred on the processing of the information to enable it to integrate both with different file outputs and with search and indexing technologies. The move to digital-first output is still ongoing at many scholarly publishers, but developments in printing technologies such as Print On Demand (POD) and Print To Order (PTO) are rapidly replacing offset printing and allowing the printed output to become a secondary product of the digital publishing process.

Traditional publishing was all about the physical output of a complete journal issue or book. As we move into the digital environment, publishing is more about the findability and usability of content which, more often than not, is segmented into pieces (chapter, article, image etc.). To this end, publishers have to alter their production processes so as to create a full-text XML output that can then be converted into multiple file types such as ePub and HTML5 for delivery to a myriad of reading devices. Users may want to read the content on a PDA, laptop, smartphone or tablet, so the content has to be flexible enough to cope with all these formats. Output in full-text XML exposes more of the content to search engines and allows for further refining of the reading environment through technologies such as semantic fingerprinting.

One example of the work being done in this area is Elsevier's Article of the Future project, which seeks to develop the article-reading environment by adapting the presentation and enriching the experience through the addition of features such as protein viewers and Google Maps. This project was developed with many partners from the academic community and underscores that, while the article-reading environment can be enriched in the digital world, the intrinsic structure of the article remains true to its traditional form. John Mackenzie Owen echoed this view in his book *The Scientific Article in the Age of Digitization*:

> Many journals failed to benefit from the possibilities of the digital format, and when they did, authors and readers in general were reluctant to utilize them, even though they used digital means for creating and acquiring scientific information. The e-only journal as an innovative format has now been largely replaced by the even more conventional format of the open access journal. The experiment, in so far as it really was aimed at transforming the scientific article has failed.[1]

Even though the traditional structure of the scientific article has not altered greatly, the way that readers search, browse, interact with and purchase content has changed dramatically with the transition to digital.

The output process

It is in the distribution, product development and business models that the transition to digital publishing has really had a major impact on how publishers work. A new subscription journal article can reach a global network of thousands of libraries and millions of readers as soon as it is published online, and OA articles have an audience restricted only by readers' ability to access the internet. This reach would have been unthinkable in print, even in the biggest scholarly journals. The same applies to scholarly books – some of which might previously have been accessible in only 100 libraries globally – which now enjoy exposure to this same global audience. This allows publishers to accept manuscripts in very niche areas of research because the new economics of e-books mean that replication and distribution is far more cost effective than it ever was with print books.

Digital hosting and distribution

For publishers, the options for digital hosting are numerous, ranging from in-house hosted content platforms such as ScienceDirect, to externally hosted platforms such as Springerlink or Metapress, to aggregated externally hosted solutions such as Highwire. Much work has been done in this area, although developments in the area of searching and discovery tools are starting to downgrade the role of these platforms to mere full-text repositories, with most of the searching being done externally. On Springerlink, 84% of full-text article requests come from a point that originated in a search engine, abstract database or a direct link from a library source (including link resolvers); thus the number of readers searching on the platform itself is relatively low. The most-used search mechanism for scholarly articles is general search engines, with Google being the most popular; however, social media are starting to play a more significant role, with sites such as Facebook starting to generate noticeable traffic.

Two major advances in search and retrieval of full-text information have been the growth of multi-platform discovery solutions such as Primo or Summon and the opening up of publisher platform API layers, which has made the independent development of custom interfaces possible. Discovery solutions are implemented on the library side and allow for a single search across multiple sources, both internal and external, and across different formats (book chapters and journal articles, for example). This is a natural progression from searching in abstract and indexing databases, which to a certain degree performed a similar function but were restricted to searching in the abstract rather than the full text. API accessibility allows for the development of new tools and enrichment solutions to be used in conjunction with the existing full-text content that is provided by the publisher. For a publisher, this means that the variety of interactions between their content and the readers keeps increasing and must be managed and supported.

The transition to digital publishing has provided many improvements in the scholarly communication process. But it has also added a level of complexity that did not exist in the print world (Figure 8.1). Picking and supporting the right paths to the users and then providing the information in formats of their choice, while also supporting an increasingly sophisticated library structure, has changed the face of the modern publisher.

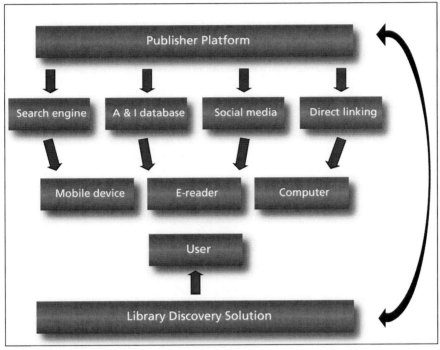

Figure 8.1 Digital content interaction between publisher, library and user

Together with the change in the way that content is distributed, there is also a shift in the way that the content is sold, in terms both of infrastructure and of the business models that have developed with the shift to digital.

In the print world, publishers relied on the services of intermediaries to get their content to where it needed to go. These intermediaries were the distribution channel to all the major libraries in the world, and quite often it was enough for publishers to promote to subscription agents as their only sales channel. The advent of digital distribution altered the geographical restrictions for publishers and allowed them to distribute content to anywhere in the world. This led to a fundamental shift in the interactions of publishers with their library customers, from indirect to direct. The digital transition also pushed the development of groups of libraries (consortia) buying electronic resources together, either in a closed consortium, where the purchase was centralized, or in an open consortium arrangement, where the terms were agreed together but individual libraries could then act independently.

This change coincided with the development of the so-called 'Big Deal' business model for buying journals. This model developed from a print subscription model and allowed libraries to pay a surcharge so as to get electronic access to their print journals. This in turn led to the development of consortial sharing of resources, where groups of libraries could purchase together and get shared access to each other's journal subscriptions in electronic form. These print and electronic combined deals developed into deals for electronic-only access and the links to the original subscriptions became less obvious. For many libraries this model increased the accessibility to journal content significantly and reduced the differences between the journal collections of large and small institutions. However, it reduced libraries' flexibility in allocating funds to new resources and so has become a point of conflict between publishers and libraries. It is this conflict, together with an ideological push towards increased accessibility to scientific research, which has fuelled much of the rise of OA as an alternative business model.

Once the published information has been digitized, organized and distributed, many users want to dig deeper into the information, using text-mining/data-mining tools. Text mining (or text data mining) treats full-text resources as large data sets and looks to either discover patterns or extract fragments of data that can be used to analyse the full-text information in a different manner. Initiatives such as the UCSC Genome Browser utilize text mining to extract very specific genomic information from large bodies of full text and present this in a central searchable data resource. These tools have the potential to uncover important relationships in scientific research that might not have been obvious through reading individual articles alone.

Conclusion: the future

Publishing has undergone unprecedented change in the past 20 years. Yet the process of scholarly communication in respect of peer review, the editorial process and structure of the communication of scientific research has yet to be truly altered. However, while the process may not have altered much, there are developments in the way in which the information is presented online. And the breakdown of the 'paper' structures such as journal issues and books as static entities will continue to evolve. Publishers will move further into a database format of publishing and continue to look at ways to extract more value from the content through developments in search technology, linking and text-mining tools. Interaction with authors and readers through social media and other digital channels will continue to develop, as recent research published in *PLoS One*[2] has shown a strong association between social media interest, article downloads and citations. This association will surely continue to grow and publishers will have to adapt, and embrace all avenues in order to bring themselves closer to their audience. This should fuel increasing dialogue, both positive and negative, that will help to push the scientific publishing environment forward.

With the disaggregation of journal content and the adaptation of reading habits to a digital environment there will be an increasing move towards article-level metrics and a focus on the individual paper rather than the journal. Impact factors at the journal level can impart a stamp of quality that can be statistically inaccurate when applied to an individual paper.[3] The rise of Altmetrics (Alternative Metrics), which uses statistics from various sources such as Twitter, Facebook, blogs and Mendeley to create an Altmetric score, will bring some much-needed article-level analytics.

Preservation of scientific research and the supporting of changing content formats will continue to be central to the role of the publisher. Adapting production processes in order to gather increasing levels of metadata so as to make content more findable is an ongoing process and will be dictated by both external search technologies and changes in the digital library environment.

Business models will continue to adapt and OA will continue to be a large discussion point, both from a publishing and a political perspective. Gold OA has shown that it can be a viable business model and it will continue to develop, especially with the help of some significant political and funding council mandates. For many publishers, it will evolve alongside traditional subscription business models and provide another way to facilitate scholarly communication.

Publishers continue to face a changing environment in terms of technology, format, accessibility and business models. They will need to rise to these new challenges in order to ensure that they have a part to play in the future scholarly communication process.

References

1 Mackenzie Owen, J. (2007) *The Scientific Article in the Age of Digitization*, Springer.

2 Shuai, X., Pepe, A. and Bollen, J. (2012) How the Scientific Community Reacts to Newly Submitted Preprints: article downloads, Twitter mentions, and citations, *PLoS One*, **7** (11), e47523. doi: 10.1371/journal.pone.0047523.

3 Vanclay, J. K. (2012) *Impact Factor: outdated artefact or stepping-stone to journal certification?* doi: 10.1007/s11192-011-0561-0.

Part 2
Other players: roles and responsibilities

9

The changing role of the journal editor

Mike McGrath

ABSTRACT

Drawing on ten years' experience as a journal editor, the author of this chapter looks at the key drivers for change in the journal market-place: the drive for profit by the large commercials and the impact of rapidly developing technology which is enabling different access and publishing models to be explored. These drivers are leading to changes in the editorial function, in particular the role of peer reviewing moving from pre- to post-publication review. The exaggeration of the added value contributed by publishers may be a matter of debate. The very significant impact of Open Access (OA) is assessed and some predictions are made, including the likely demise of the Big Deal, at least in its present form, because of the impact of OA. The chapter concludes by arguing that publishers have contributed greatly to increasing access to the academic literature but are now acting as a brake on further developments through their exploitation of copyright law and digital rights management constraints. All these factors will see the role of the journal editor change dramatically in the next five to ten years, more quickly in the fields of science, technology and medicine, and more slowly in the humanities and social sciences.

Introduction

'As long as the journal remains important for the achievement of research funding and tenure, it will endure as a key component of scholarly communication';[1] and, as David Worlock notes on his blog: 'the science knowledge market is in a ferment'.[2] Changes taking place today are subverting the business models of journals and threatening the stability of the tenure system; the role of the journal editor is bound up with these changes.

The journals industry is very large; globally, there are about 225,000 active journals, of which 63,000 are academic journals, with 25,000 seen as core titles; these estimates are discussed by Tenopir and King.[3] Changing the course of an industry of this size, rather like turning an oil tanker round, is a slow and complex process, which makes prediction difficult. However, some emerging trends will dramatically affect the roles of both journals and their editors. Traditionally, the key functions of a journal editor are to provide the publisher with a regular supply of articles, usually in a particular discipline, and of a satisfactory quality. These functions and how they are changing or disappearing in a market 'in ferment' will be considered in this chapter. But first a personal take; and to follow, some comments on the strange nature of the academic journal and the key drivers for change.

A personal take

I edited *Interlending & Document Supply* for ten years, until the end of 2011. I received excellent support from the staff at the publisher – Emerald – and was treated with unfailing courtesy and competence. That said, I felt that I had little or no influence on important issues such as pricing, about which I and many other editors (not just from Emerald) complain repeatedly; indeed, some editors have resigned in protest over pricing. The downloads from the journal trebled over the ten years; not, I suspect, as a result of my brilliant editorship, as many other journals in the Emerald stable showed similar increases. Rather, this increase was due mainly to the Big Deals widening access, together with an improved format for abstracts and better indexing. The productivity and efficiency of the editorial function has dramatically improved since the pre-electronic days when I edited journals in the 1970s and 1980s. For example, I recall a journal that I edited in the early 1970s for which I also created the 'artwork'; this involved cutting up columns of text that had been produced by a professional typist on an electric golf-ball typewriter and pasting the resulting pieces on card for the printer to make a photographic plate. The editor was the conduit for manuscripts, and when these came from abroad there could be weeks of delay: an article requiring four or five iterations could take months to complete. Truly an age ago! Today communications and the editing process are fast, efficient and conducted entirely from the desktop. However, the functions of an editor have remained largely the same. This 'happy' state will not continue for much longer, as I shall explain below.

The strangeness of the journal

The producers of a journal – authors, reviewers and editors – provide their services free of charge, although an editor may receive a modest honorarium. Individual consumers, who are also often producers, read for free – the librarian pays the publisher, who has added some value in the process, but by no means as much as the producers have. This is a very strange business model, and one that is now under considerable strain. Indeed it is breaking up, partly as a result of monopolistic pricing practices and partly because of the rise of Open Access (OA), which in turn is generating different business models as commercial publishers, in particular, try to head off disaster.

Key drivers for change

There are two key drivers for change in the journal market-place. First and most important is the commercial publishers' drive to maximize their rate of return on investment, or profit. They do this by driving down costs – hence digitization and software to reduce expensive labour costs – and driving up revenue – hence monopolization and Big Deals, leading to high prices. Second is technology, facilitating new forms of scholarly communication which can both enhance profits and at the same time annihilate them as institutional repositories grow bigger and better. This trend could even lead to the demise of science, technology and medicine (STM) journals and many others, along with their editors and associated workers.

The editorial function

Peer review – essential or outmoded?

'Looking at it as dispassionately as possible, one could conclude that peer review is the only remaining significant *raison d'être* of formal scientific publishing in journals.' Thus wrote Jan Velterop in his blog.[4]

A debate ensued, leading to some agreement that post-publication reviewing is both better and cheaper. This view is supported by the ex-editor of the *British Medical Journal* – 'I see four main objectives for peer review: selecting what should be published, improving what is published, detecting errors, and detecting fraud' – who comments further:

> The problem with filtering before publishing, peer review, is that it is an ineffective, slow, expensive, biased, inefficient, anti-innovatory, and easily abused lottery: the important is just as likely to be filtered out as the unimportant. The sooner we can let the 'real' peer review of post-publication peer review get to work the better.[5]

Reviewers are an unpaid and unsung army who labour without monetary reward, motivated, in the main, by a sense of professional duty. Currently the editor selects the reviewers on the basis of recommendation or personal knowledge. The problem for the author, and indeed for the reader, is that the reviewing process is not transparent and can be influenced by many subjective factors, of which Cope and Kalantzis provide a comprehensive critique.[6] An even more disturbing analysis of the quality of articles published under the current practice has been made by Young, Ioannidis and Al-Ubaydli.[7] To note just one of their arguments, a rejection rate of 90% for *Nature* says more about the inadequacy of the publishing system than it does about the quality of the articles. 'Manuscripts are assessed with a fundamentally negative bias: how they may best be *rejected* to promote the presumed selectivity of the journal. Journals closely track and advertise their low acceptance rates, equating these with rigorous review.' But the situation is changing: post-publication reviewing is growing in a number of disciplines. Articles are scanned briefly before publication, and out-of-scope or obviously poor ones are rejected; reviewing then relies on post-publication feedback. This process has been encouraged by the successful example of Wikipedia – written and post-publication reviewed for free, but nonetheless compared favourably with the expensive *Encyclopaedia Britannica*.[8] And in an interview Timo Hannay from *Nature* stated: 'My personal view is that peer review is headed for a revolution at some point, but the timing is extremely difficult to predict because it depends mainly not on technology but on various interdependent and imponderable social factors.' And: 'I ... believe that the web is particularly well suited to a "publish then filter" approach rather than the traditional "filter then publish" approach that was required when publishing was necessarily a physical-world process.'[9] In this context, F1000 Research is a well-funded service to watch. Launched in early 2012, it will publish immediately in OA and review post-publication. The process is worth quoting, as it is succinct, sensible and widely applicable:

> Open, post-publication peer review. This means no closed editorial decisions based on personal biases or subjective views of possible impact. Review will be a simple formal check by invited reviewers confirming that the work is scientifically sound, with commenting optional. At this and any stage following deposition of the work, any registered reader can also comment on the work and authors can respond. An 'approved' or 'not approved' stamp with the invited reviewers' name(s) and comments will then accompany the article.[10]

Thus the important role of peer reviewing, currently managed by the editor, is replaced by 'the wisdom of crowds'. Initiatives such as this, which are practical, sensible and respond to the need for faster publication as well as being very cheap will grow fast in the next few years, with dramatic consequences for the highly priced journals market, whose function may well be reduced to expensive career-progression artefacts. And of course *arXiv* has required endorsement of papers combined with post-reviewing since 2004. However, some have reservations, such as Steven Harnad, who notes that 'The critical difference [between pre- and post-publication reviewing] is *answerability*. An author is answerable to the editor for meeting the referee's recommendations. With *post hoc* commentary, whether or not to meet commentators' recommendations is entirely up to the author.'[11] Harnad also raises the issue of the qualification of such reviewers to undertake the task – a point addressed by F1000 Research. A significant move to post-publication reviewing will have a dramatic impact on journals and the role of their editors. Indeed, why bother with the journal at all if you, as an author, simply want wide distribution and access? Instead just send your article to an appropriate repository and invite critical comment.

Attracting appropriate articles

Contrary to Jan Velterop's assertion that peer review is the only justification for scientific journals, the most enduring function of an editor, and hence of the journal itself, is to attract appropriate articles. Even if 100% of academic outputs were in freely accessible repositories there would still be a strong case for selecting material from those outputs, with the help of post-publication reviewing, and then packaging them into a journal targeted at a specific audience. In addition, a good editor will not be simply a passive recipient of manuscripts but will be on the look-out for emerging trends likely to be of interest to readers and will commission authors who are best placed to write appropriate articles. Technology has vastly improved the quality of this process. Editors can jump instantly around the world – from a university in China to a medical research centre in the UK to CERN in Switzerland; from conference proceedings to PowerPoint presentations, blogs, interviews and monographs; and all this from their desktop.

There aren't many certainties in this world – only death and taxes, opined Benjamin Franklin; a librarian might add information overload. But how to deal with it? We need filters – but who selects the filters, and how? How do researchers choose filters when they don't always know what they are looking for? Anyone else doing the filtering might filter out useful stuff. And 'you chose that, you might like this' is less useful when the subject is multi-disciplinary; in any event, at best it is pretty crude and at worst a waste of time. The editors earn their keep here: many proposed articles can be filtered out at an early stage prior to peer review, on the grounds of either quality or appropriateness. Even after peer review editors and their boards must still select, sometimes ruthlessly, if the journal is very popular.

A note on journal costs

Currently a journal editor usually delivers final, agreed texts of articles, including editorials, letters etc., to the publisher's website using special software and allocates the material to specific issues of the journal. The software converts the texts to HTML and PDF formats for processing by the publisher. The same software allows the editor to manage the peer-review process. This is simply done where rejection rates are low, but more labour intensive where rates of rejection are high. Thus, contrary to the impression given by some publishers, it is the *editor*, not the publisher, who manages the vital peer-review process. Many publishers justify the high price of their journals by citing the costs of peer reviewing and editing. Their justification is simply not true: authors and peer reviewers write and comment without payment, and hence the cost to the publisher is trivial or zero. The editor organizes the material into a finished issue at little cost to the publisher. The publisher's costs start after submission of the finished journal part and can be attributed primarily to typesetting, indexing and distribution. They also spend money on IT and marketing, but whether their high prices are justified by these and other essential costs is, to say the least, controversial.

The transformation of the article

A good case can be made for claiming that the journal is becoming irrelevant, especially in STM research. We are close to seeing the integration of research data – images, data files, correspondence etc. – into a single, dynamic object. This can be made accessible worldwide to all relevant researchers for feedback leading to formal peer review of an 'article' with associated metadata. It can then be published as a holistic account of the current state of research in a particular area. A well-produced presentation illustrating Elsevier's vision of this process has been provided by de Waard.[12]

The role of the reviewer and editor in this context could become more onerous (with more material to review), but would be eased by the shift towards post-publication reviewing. The role of the journal as the aggregator of formally published articles would become less critical:

> Instead of a lock-step march to a single point of publication, then a near-irrevocable fixity to the published record, a more incremental process of knowledge recording and refinement is straightforwardly possible in the digital era. This could even end the distinction between pre-publication refereeing and post-publication review ... thus opening the published text to continuous improvement.[4]

In the latter, the editor becomes rather like the Cheshire Cat in *Alice in Wonderland*, as their function gradually disappears – although not quite with the

Cat's grin. The speed of the transformation will depend on the discipline – life sciences, and indeed any disciplines that generate large amounts of data, are already changing rapidly. The editor may well become more important as the arbiter of when an article of record is produced. Indeed we may see more articles produced as reviewing leads to further iterations of the original article and perhaps to further research, leading to even more articles.

An additional role for the editor in an electronic environment where articles and research data do not sit in the silo of a journal (usually behind a pay wall) is to draw attention to a published article's relevance to another field. Freed from the boundaries of copyright constraint as OA develops, interdisciplinary cross-fertilization may increase. For example, mathematical developments apply across many disciplines – fuzzy logic can be used for integrating fragments of ancient papyri, creating stellar corpuses and even the priorities for kidney transplants. Editors could become a new freebooting fraternity facilitating the free trade in ideas and knowledge across disciplines, journals and national boundaries.

Scholars will reward the journals whose editorial boards gather experimental data, graphs and comments related to the solution of common problems, forming optimal discourses on a specific issue. By taking them to the limit of their possibilities, these journals will give the best of themselves in this digital era, an era we have yet barely entered. Scientists will … not complain if their articles are published by several journals at the same time. On the contrary, they will be delighted.[13]

Indeed revised versions could be produced for different journals or repositories at different times for different purposes. The role of the pro-active editor should be all important in this exciting process.

The impact of OA

Timo Hannay believes that 'Open access will come about mainly through funder-mandated self-archiving, not author- or sponsor-funded journals',[7] and he poses the question (without answering it) of 'how to create viable business models that don't involve charging for content (whether readers or authors)'. However, in the short term OA is having little impact on editors: because their function is to deliver high-quality content for publication, they are not interested in how this material is accessed and paid for. (Of course the editor *is* interested in OA. It has a significant impact on hit rates and impact factors, and hence on the long-term health of their journal. And they may also have a moral commitment to free access.) But the *method* of access is not under their control and does not affect what they do. It is for the publisher to decide how to at least cover costs and, in the case of a commercial publisher, how to make sufficient profits to satisfy the shareholders. However, in the longer term (five to ten years) OA is likely to have a fundamental impact. As accepted articles are sent to repositories and increasing numbers of published articles are no longer embargoed, the very existence of the journal as an artefact for bundling articles will be threatened. But this process will occur over a long timescale and will vary enormously depending upon the subject discipline. For example, 90% of articles in the 15 most-cited economics journals can be found freely – although 'only' 50% of them in less-cited journals.[14] In a 2008 study the percentage of OA articles for much of astronomy, computer science, high-energy physics and mathematics was found to be about 20%, and for earth sciences it was 26%. These last two figures seem low, but evidence is scarce – most of it concentrated on the citation-rate controversy.[15] My own experience in library and information science (LIS) is that around 50% of the material that I cover in my quarterly literature review is easily, freely and immediately available on the web – an increase of about 25% over a five-year period. Given this growth, the large majority of articles will probably be freely available to readers within 10–15 years.

So long as a key metric for tenure and advancement remains the journal article, the journal will continue to exist, albeit in an etiolated form; unless, of course, publishers can successfully manage a transition to author-side payments. But these fees are currently set so high (often £2,000 and more per article) that they are affordable only by researchers in well-funded projects. Thus, OA via repositories may well be the subversive factor that undermines the existence of the journal and the academic assessment process as currently formulated. The journal editors will be casualties of this process, although not their functions, which will still be needed in order to ensure that research results are published and that sufficient quality assurance is maintained. Their relationship will then be with repositories rather than with journals as artefacts. It is amusing to reflect that the wheel will have then turned full circle: universities and other research bodies may once again become the key sources of publication and distribution. This was, after all, what happened before Robert Maxwell struck a Faustian bargain with university and society presses in the 1950s and 1960s and commercialized the production of academic journals in the UK through his Pergamon Press (now part of Elsevier).

An interesting consequence of OA is that conference proceedings are likely to increase in importance. Once highly inaccessible, they have been transformed by technology. So editors in this area may well become more important, encouraging authors to revise papers delivered at conferences, or indeed to write papers in the first place instead of just making PowerPoint presentations.

OA has dealt a fatal blow to the subscription model; but, like James Cagney in *The Public Enemy* or Caesar at the Ides of March, the model will take a long time to die. New actors are entering the stage: Green, Gold, Hybrid, Delayed access etc. However, who will be left standing at the curtain call is still not clear.

The pace of change?

From a reading of the LIS literature you might think that the future of scholarly communications in journals is determined by research activity in the fields of STM. These fields are at the forefront of change, but there are limits to that change. Articles published in medicine and some science and technology fields are written by well-funded researchers who can afford to pay author-side fees for OA publication. A cancer researcher can pay such fees, but a medieval historian may well not be in the same position. The latter is also unlikely to need the software, and indeed hardware, to store and manage very large data sets such as are generated by the medical researcher, although even here the digitization of manuscripts and incunabula (pre-1500 books) has transformed access to primary sources. The humanities and social sciences (HSS) are slower moving than STM, hence the speed of the publication process is less important (and there is more potential for book publication, although this is declining), at least in the academic sector. So the drivers for change vary in importance, depending on the subject matter. At one end of the spectrum an electronic object capable of constant revision and containing gigabytes of data and images with dynamic revisions is rapidly transforming scholarly communications; at the other end a conventionally produced article, mainly in electronic format and still predominantly published in subscription journals, will continue for many years, supported by traditional editors, albeit working differently in the light of technical developments.

The future of the journal and the editor

The oil tanker *SS Academic Publishing* is turning slowly, under pressure from pricing protests and the growing number of authors depositing their publications in open access repositories (Green OA). But the rocks on which it will founder are nearly unavoidable, and there will be few survivors. Why should institutions spend vast sums buying back the work of their members when an increasing proportion of it can be obtained freely and easily via institutional or subject repositories? And reviewing can be done post- rather than pre-publication, along the lines of F1000 Research (see above). Take, for example, LIS – familiar to most readers of this book. It will be much easier to set up current-awareness searches based on linked and/or subject repositories rather than on numerous publishers – few of which can be accessed without payment (Routledge, Emerald, Elsevier etc.). How long will this process take? The UK higher education community signed a five-year deal with Elsevier and Wiley in 2011 which may well be the last of the Big Deals. By 2016 a very high proportion of material will be freely available, as long as the academic and research community globally follows a strategy of developing and populating repositories.

Will any journals survive this process? Yes, as suggested above; many professional societies will continue to publish, although not at prices that currently subsidize their other activities. Many HSS journals will survive for longer, some indefinitely. And of course generic journals for the wider community – *Nature, Science, New Scientist, Scientific American* – will also continue indefinitely. But the STM market dominated by the large commercial publishers will not. Editorial skills will survive, but they will be focused on repositories, selecting, quality assuring, reviewing etc.

Conclusion

In this current ferment editorial skills will remain important in scientific 'publication'; but in future these skills will be distributed increasingly across many individuals, none of whom is likely to be called an editor. The days are numbered for editors who remain at the passive end of the spectrum, waiting for authors to approach them with manuscripts. This will happen sooner in STM subjects, particularly those with heavy financial investment and large data sets, than in HSS disciplines. Even here there is potential to link with and integrate large amounts of relevant older material within current articles – a potential that goes far beyond the simple 'hot linking' of URLs. The key constraint is the role of the publisher and the fetters of copyright. Relevant here is Karl Marx's insight that the old economic system has outlived its usefulness but has not yet been supplanted by the new. In our context the commercial publishers have not yet been supplanted by repositories.

In 1900 another socialist, Rosa Luxemburg, wrote *Reform or Revolution?* in which she argued for revolution. (She was murdered for her commitment.) But her fundamental question remains one of the hardest to answer, whether in politics or in the more mundane field of knowledge working. We can hazard that both reform and revolution will occur in knowledge generation, at varying speeds depending on the discipline: faster and more revolutionary in STM subjects, slower and more reformist in HSS. In the longer term – perhaps within 20 years – we shall probably see a convergence of all disciplines in a 'socialist utopia' where the results of all research are freely and easily accessible to all, with all the benefits of cross-fertilization that this will bring. In this utopia the skills of the editor to commission, filter and organize will still be needed. But the production of most journal titles will almost certainly be confined to the wider consumer market and the humanities.

Further reading

- David Dobbs provides a useful summary of the tools and initiatives both in place and under development and that have potential for replacing the current journal system: www.wired.com/wiredscience/ 2012/02/is-the-open-science-revolution-for-real.
- An excellent aggregation of current and not-so-current contributions (immensely useful and fascinating) to reforming the present publishing system is at: http://michaelnielsen.org/polymath1/ index.php?title=Journal_publishing_reform.
- Richard Poynder's website is always interesting:

http://richardpoynder.co.uk. See in particular the interviews with Alicia Wise of Elsevier and Jan Velterop, the OA guru; also the interview with Michael Eisen, editor of PLoS One and co-founder of the Public Library of Science.

References

1 Cope, B. and Philips, A. (2009) *The Future of the Academic Journal*, Chandos.
2 www.davidworlock.com/2012/02/the-point-of-utility.
3 Tenopir, C. and King, D. W. (2009) The Growth of Journal Publishing. In: Cope, B. and Philips, A. (eds) *The Future of the Academic Journal*, Chandos.
4 http://theparachute.blogspot.com/2012/01/holy-cow-peer-review.html.
5 Smith, R. (2010), Classical Peer Review: an empty gun, *Breast Cancer Research*, **12** (Suppl 4), S13, http://breast-cancer-research.com/content/12/S4/S13.
6 Cope, B. and Kalantzis, M. (2009) In: Cope, B. and Philips, A. (eds) *The Future of the Academic Journal*, Chandos.
7 Young, N. S., Ioannidis, N. P. A. and Al-Ubaydli, O. (2008) Why Current Publication Practices May Distort Science, *PloS Medicine*, **5** (10), www.plosmedicine.org/article/info%3Adoi%2F10.1371%2Fjournal.pmed.0050201.
8 Giles, J. (2005) Special Report: internet encyclopaedias go head to head, *Nature*, **438**, (15 December), 900–901.
9 Hannay, T. (2007) Interview with Timo Hannay, Head of Web Publishing, Nature Publishing Group, http://scienceblogs.com/confessions/2009/08/from_the_archives_interview_wi.php.
10 http://f1000research.com/2012/01/30/f1000-research-join-us-and-shape-the-future-of-scholarly-communication-2.
11 Harnad, S. (2009) The Post-Gutenberg Open Access Journal. In: Cope, B. and Philips, A. (eds) *The Future of the Academic Journal*, Chandos.
12 de Waard, A. (2010) *The Future of the Journal*, www.slideshare.net/anitawaard/the-future-of-the-journal.
13 Quirós, J. L. G. and Gherab, K. (2009) Arguments for an Open Model of E-science. In: Cope, B. and Philips, A. (eds) *The Future of the Academic Journal*, Chandos.
14 Bergstrom, T. and Lavaty, R. (2007) *How often Do Economists Self-archive?* www.escholarship.org/uc/item/69f4b8vz#page-1.
15 For more details see http://en.wikipedia.org/wiki/Open_access.

10

The view of the research funder

Robert Kiley

ABSTRACT

This chapter considers the benefits of Open Access (OA), the challenges that still persist – especially in terms of compliance with funders' policies – and the costs and sustainability of OA publishing, with particular reference to the work of the Wellcome Trust since 2005. To provide context to the Trust's initiatives, a brief analysis of the OA landscape in the UK, Europe and beyond is also provided. The chapter also discusses the rationale behind the development of eLife, the new OA journal developed by the Wellcome Trust in collaboration with the Howard Hughes Medical Institute and the Max Planck Society.

Introduction

A study in 2011 estimated that for every $1 that the US government invested in the human genome project, $141 of economic activity was generated.[1] As one of the sponsors study observed, 'from a simple return on investment, the financial stake made in mapping the entire human genome is clearly one of the best uses of taxpayer dollars the U.S. government has ever made'.[2]

This single example demonstrates the benefits that can be reaped from open content, and explains why it is logical for research funders to develop policies that require the outputs of the research they fund to be made freely available, for both humans and machines to read and make use of. Stated simply, it makes absolutely no sense from a return-on-investment perspective for a funder to invest in research but then allow the outputs of that research – most typically the research articles published in peer-reviewed journals – to remain hidden behind publishers' pay walls.

With reference to the work of the Wellcome Trust, this chapter considers the benefits of Open Access (OA), the challenges that still persist – especially in terms of compliance with funders' policies – and the costs and sustainability of OA publishing. To provide context to the Trust's initiatives, a brief analysis of the OA landscape in the UK, Europe and beyond will also be provided. The chapter will also discuss the rationale behind the development of *eLife*, the new OA journal developed by the Wellcome Trust in collaboration with the Howard Hughes Medical Institute and the Max Planck Society.

OA: the Wellcome Trust's policy

The need to rethink the way scholarly communications are conducted became abundantly clear shortly after the appointment of Mark Walport as Director of the Wellcome Trust in 2002. In what can now be described as a *cause célèbre*, the new Director tried to access a research paper[3] on the web that had been jointly funded by the Trust and the Medical Research Council. However, as the Wellcome Library did not hold a subscription to the journal in question, he could gain access only by flourishing a credit card and agreeing to a $30 fee.

The folly of this situation was evident on a number of levels. First, the two funding bodies had already invested significant resources into the research, and so being asked to pay again just seemed wrong. Second, and more significantly, *other* non-subscribers – researchers, clinicians, patients and industry-based personnel – could not access this article without paying the $30 fee. Since the article focused on malaria vaccines, it seemed particularly unfortunate that many of the people engaged in trying to combat the disease could not gain access to it.

As a result of this case, and following the commissioning of two studies[4] into the scholarly publishing market, the Wellcome Trust in 2005 became the world's first research funder to announce an OA policy.

The policy: a summary

The Wellcome Trust's policy is simple.[5] In just over 300 words it laid the foundation for changing the way in which scholarly communication operated. Specifically, the policy stated that all research papers that have been accepted for publication in a peer-reviewed journal and are supported in whole or in part by Wellcome Trust funding must be made available through PubMed Central (PMC) and UK PubMed Central (UKPMC) as soon as possible, and in any event within six months of the journal publisher's official date of final publication.

In addition to this very clear mandate, the policy also included three other crucial elements.

First, it made clear that the Trust would provide grant-holders with additional funding (through their institutions) to cover OA publication charges. Although the Trust imposed conditions on publishers who wished to take advantage of this – specifically a requirement that the publisher undertake the deposit of the final version of the article in UKPMC, where it must be made freely available at the time of publication – this approach is in accord with the view that dissemination costs are research costs, and as such should be met by the research funder.

Second, the policy required those publishers who levied an OA fee to license research papers so that they may be freely copied and reused (including for text and data mining), subject only to attribution of the authors and publication. In June 2012 the Trust updated this aspect of the policy[6] to specify that when an OA fee is charged such works must be accessible under the Creative Commons, Attribution licence (CC-BY).[7]

Third, the Trust affirmed 'the principle that it is the intrinsic merit of the work, and not the title of the journal in which an author's work is published, that should be considered in making funding decisions'. Although this element of the policy has attracted relatively little interest, it is a key principle that has allowed researchers to seek publication in whichever journal they deem suitable, knowing that future funding decisions will be based on the value of their work, not where they have published it.

OA: UK, Europe and beyond

Although the Wellcome Trust was the first research funder to make OA a condition of grant, research funders around the world were beginning to recognize the potential benefits that OA could deliver.

Research Councils UK

In 2005 the UK Research Councils (RCUK) published a position statement on OA.[8] This set out four key principles, central to which was the notion that 'ideas and knowledge derived from publicly-funded research are made available and accessible for public use, interrogation, and scrutiny, as widely, rapidly and effectively as practicable'. In order to clarify issues relating to the author-pays model, RCUK stated in 2006 that it was up to the 'authors' institutions to decide whether they are prepared to use funds for any page charges or other publishing fees'.[9]

The statement indicated some tensions between the approach of different Councils, and the Medical Research Council (MRC) shortly afterwards updated its guidance, stating that 'The MRC will pay any necessary charges levied by publishers who offer Open Access options, providing these have been included under Directly Incurred Costs on grant proposals and where these costs fall within the period of the grant. Anticipated future publication costs (Author Pays charges) should be part of an institution's indirect costs under the full economic costing regime'.[10] In 2008, the BBSRC (Biotechnology and Biological Sciences Research Council) adopted a similar approach.[11]

Since 2006, there has been much activity around OA in the UK, but there was relatively little development of policy until the publication of the Finch Report in 2012.[12] Its key recommendation was that 'a clear policy direction should be set towards support for publication in open access or hybrid journals, funded by article processing charges (APCs), as the main vehicle for the publication of research, especially when it is publicly funded'. In light of the report, RCUK revised its policy,[13] announcing, most significantly, its intention to meet the cost of OA publication fees by awarding block grants to UK higher education institutions (HEIs). No longer would researchers have to identify publication costs in their grants, nor would HEIs have to budget for this expense as an indirect cost. This development has the potential to play a significant role in accelerating the transition to OA, both in the UK and beyond.

OA in Europe

Across Europe, many research funders have also adopted OA policies. There is no space to discuss all of them here, but a good summary can be found on the OpenAire website.[14] The European Commission introduced a 'pilot' OA policy[15] under its Framework 7 programme in 2008. This specifies that for certain areas – including health, environment and energy – research outputs have to be made OA within 6 or 12 months of publication (depending upon the discipline).

The Commission is still discussing what the OA policy will look like for the next framework programme (known as Horizon 2020), but early indications suggest that the OA mandate will be applied to all EU-funded research.

OA in the United States

Policy on OA in the USA has been led by the National Institutes of Health (NIH), which published a draft policy[16] in 2004 requiring all NIH-funded research to be made freely available through PubMed Central (PMC) within six months of publication. This proposal generated a huge amount of comment – mainly from publishers who argued that their business model would be undermined by a six-month embargo – and by the time the policy was finalized in February 2005, researchers were asked only to deposit papers 'as soon as possible (and within twelve months of publication)'.

The policy was thus not a mandate but a 'request' to NIH grant holders to make their work available through PMC. Researchers who did not comply with this request were not penalized in any way. Deposit rates were low – around 4% – and hence in 2007 Congress approved a Bill which *required* all NIH-funded research to be made available through PMC within 12 months of publication. As a result around 75% of NIH-funded research is now publicly accessible through PMC.[17]

The success of the NIH policy has led other federal agencies to consider following suit. The Federal Research Public Access Act,[18] re-introduced into the House of Representatives in March 2012, would, if implemented, require federal agencies with annual research budgets of $100 million or more to provide public access to this research no later than six months after publication. Whether the Bill will be enacted remains unclear; but it is clear that there is real momentum for OA throughout the world – especially in research-intensive countries like the UK and the USA – and the question now is not *will* OA become more widely adopted, but *when*.

Benefits of OA

Benefit 1: greater visibility

Papers that can be accessed without any barrier *are* more visible than those that sit behind pay walls. Indeed, research by Davis[19] showed that in a controlled trial OA articles enjoyed 95% more downloads than those that were not freely available. There is no consensus on whether more downloads leads to more citations; but there can be little doubt that there is a huge demand for research papers that is simply not being met through the current subscription model. All publishers record large numbers of 'turn-aways', and JSTOR – which is primarily an online archive of scholarly journals in the arts and humanities – has stated that in a single year it turns away almost 150 million individual attempts to gain access to articles.[20] The figure must be much higher for papers in the health-related disciplines.

Small and medium enterprises would also benefit from greater access to published material. A report published by JISC[21] in 2011 showed how companies would benefit from reduced costs, less wasted time and shortened development cycles by having greater access to research outputs, while a report in *Nature Biotechnology* laments the poor access that biotech companies have to the published literature.[22] This latter paper reports on a company that suffered 'a six-month setback to a drug development programme because a paper was missed in an inaccessible journal'. Such delays are in no one's interests.

Benefit 2: research process enhanced

Another benefit of OA is its potential to enhance the research process. An example of this can be seen in the Evidence Finder application[23] at UKPMC, through which developers at the National Centre for Text Mining have been able to extract around 10 million facts from the literature (genes, proteins, diseases and metabolites) to help researchers locate information that they might otherwise miss. Figure 10.1 shows the results page from the query 'What does BRCA2 interact with?' Rather than merely listing relevant articles, Evidence Finder extracts the relevant sentence(s) so that users can quickly determine whether the article appears to be relevant or not.

This application works because all OA articles can be freely downloaded from the UKPMC site (http://ukpmc.ac.uk/ftp/oa). The UKPMC

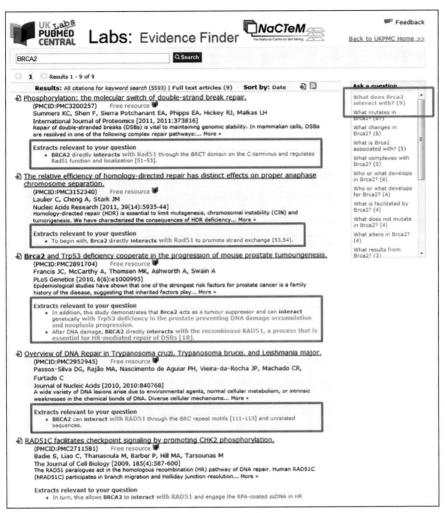

Figure 10.1 Results page in UKPMC Evidence Finder

Funders Group is keen to encourage researchers to develop their own text-mining applications which, if suitable, can then be shared with others via the UKPMC platform.

When papers are made available under a CC-BY licence they can also be used to create new, derivative products. Papers arising from the Wellcome Trust's research into malaria, for example, could be more useful if they were translated into, say, Burmese so that the information could be understood and applied in the local context; and the organization doing the translation might wish to charge for creating such a 'value added' derivative product. Under a CC-BY licence that type of commercial development is feasible.

Benefit 3: cost savings

A third benefit of OA is the potential to reduce the overall cost of scholarly communication. A 2011 study commissioned by the Research Information Network[24] suggests that a significant shift towards Gold OA – the system under which journals are funded by author-side charges rather than by subscriptions – has the potential to achieve a high benefit to cost ratio and reduce the UK's net costs for scholarly communication: if average APCs were set at about £1450, then UK universities would benefit from annual net savings of around £2.8 million.

Of course, as the study makes clear, there would be additional costs as the system transitioned from a subscription to an author-pays model, but, given the potential for cost savings – as well as the other benefits highlighted here – then there is a strong case for supporting and funding such a transition.

Compliance with OA mandate: Wellcome Trust case study

Despite the Wellcome Trust's policies and its support for OA, it is still not the case that all Trust-funded research is now freely available through UKPMC. Although compliance rates have increased steadily over the last four years, the current level of compliance is around 55% (Figure 10.2).

This level of compliance is particularly disappointing, given that some 98% of the journals in which Wellcome authors typically publish have policies fully in accord with the Trust's and that, more importantly, the Trust provides additional funding to cover APCs. Hence the Trust is introducing the following arrangements:

- In final grant reports principal investigators' institutions will be required to provide assurance that all papers associated with the grant comply with the Trust's policy. If not, the final payment on the grant will be withheld.

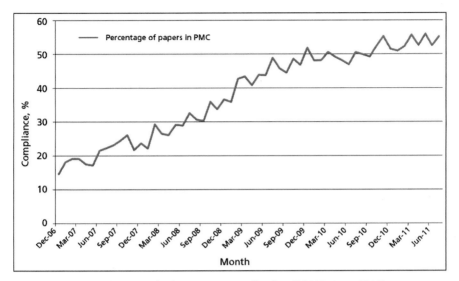

Figure 10.2 Compliance with the Trust's OA policy (April 2007–June 2011)

- Non-compliant publications will be discounted as part of Trust-funded researchers' track record in any application for renewal of an existing grant or for a new grant.
- Trust-funded researchers will be required to ensure that all publications associated with their research are compliant with the Trust's policy before any funding renewals or new grant awards will be activated.

These measures seek to change researchers' behaviour so that making research outputs OA becomes the default. The current situation – in which around 45% of the research that Wellcome funds is not made available through UKPMC – is simply not acceptable.

Researcher behaviour and OA

A 2009 survey of some 40,000 researchers[25] found that over 90% believed that OA is (or would be) beneficial for their field of research. The Wellcome Trust's experience, however, suggests that researchers are not as committed as their funders to making their own work OA. I suggest that there are three key factors in play here.

First, funds to cover APCs need to be easily accessible. The SOAP survey referenced above found that the main barrier was funding. Of course, it is possible to make research OA without paying an APC, by depositing the accepted manuscript in a subject or institutional repository (the so-called 'green' route). However, leaving aside all the arguments about the benefits of 'green' vs 'gold', the simple fact is that researchers do not routinely deposit their papers. Indeed, 89% of the Wellcome Trust-funded content that is deposited in PMC and UKPMC is deposited by publishers, typically in return for Wellcome's paying an APC. The Wellcome experience suggests that this is the most effective way to achieve OA.

Second, the processes both for depositing papers in repositories and for OA publishing – particularly in hybrid journals – are still far too complex. Often with hybrid journals – those which offer an OA option for individual articles, while still publishing under a subscription model – authors have to hunt around publishers' sites in order to find the OA option, and publishers' systems for processing OA articles are often clumsy. Many of the big commercial publishing houses, along with intermediaries who manage the payment of APCs, are now seeking to address these issues.

Third, the benefits of OA have not been fully articulated or demonstrated. For many researchers who, thanks to their library, already enjoy good access to the literature, the effort involved in making their research OA is too high for what they perceive as little return. All research funders need to devote more efforts to demonstrating the benefits of OA, for researchers themselves as well as for society at large.

Costs and sustainability

The success of publishers such as PLoS,[26] BioMed Central[27] and Hindawi[28] demonstrates that OA publishing funded by APCs does make for a sustainable business model. It is still the case, of course, that OA constitutes less than 10% of the total published output. If we are to move to a position where all research articles are made OA, then the money currently spent on library subscriptions needs to be diverted to meet APCs and the additional costs of transition. But research funders also have a role to play.

In 2010 the Wellcome Trust carried out a small study[29] to determine the costs of publishing every research paper attributed to the Trust under a Gold OA model. It showed that for the 440 OA articles published in the last quarter of 2010, the average APC was $2367, and the mode $3000. This suggests that for all the 5000 research papers attributed to the Trust and published in a single year the total cost would be around $11.8 million. Since the Trust spends around $1 billion a year on research, this represents less than 1.25% of its annual research spend. To use the language of the Occupy movement,[30] by spending just 1% of its funds on dissemination, the Trust is helping to ensure that *everyone* can access and use these outputs.

eLife

Over the last ten years the OA landscape has changed almost beyond recognition. In 2002, when the first Budapest Open Access Initiative (BOAI) declaration was published,[31] no OA funder mandates were in place, there were very few OA journals and the hybrid publishing model had not been born. By 2012 the picture was very different. The Directory of Open Access Journals lists over 8000 titles, *PLoS One* is the biggest journal on the planet and all major funders (at least in the life sciences) have OA policies.

One area, however, that has remained largely immune to OA is the top tier journals, such as *Cell*, *Nature* and *Science* (the 'CNS' journals). And, though it is true that *Nature* and *Science* allow self-archiving of author manuscripts at six months (and that *Cell* has a hybrid OA option), these titles have not fully embraced OA and hence much of the content published in them remains inaccessible to those who have not paid a subscription (or had one paid on their behalf).

In order to provide an OA alternative to the CNS titles, the Wellcome Trust, in partnership with the Howard Hughes Medical Institute and the Max Planck Society, has established *eLife*,[32] which was launched in late 2012. The new journal is fully OA, with no barriers to anyone across the world who wishes to access or reuse the research it publishes. It is entirely online, since that is the best way of delivering and preserving content globally and allows for greater innovation in the presentation and handling of data, adding more value to publications. *eLife* is also seeking to develop an editorial process that reduces revision cycles and accelerates the publication of new findings.

The development of *eLife* reflects the belief of many research funders and scientists that publishers are not adapting quickly enough to exploit the opportunities offered by today's technology.

Conclusion

Scholarly communication is undergoing a massive transformation. Initially the call for change was championed by librarians concerned at the year-on-year, inflation-busting rises in the cost of journal subscriptions; but the need for change has been recognized by many stakeholders, including researchers, policy makers and funders.

Proof that OA is now mainstream can be seen, for example, in the raft of OA journals that have been launched since 2011[33] and in the UK government's statement accepting the recommendations of the Finch Report, in particular that publication in OA or hybrid journals should be the main vehicle for the publication of research.[34]

The Wellcome Trust and other research funders have played a key role in catalysing support for change, arguing that the traditional subscription-based model is no longer working in the best interests of science or society. A better future for scholarly communication is now within our reach. We simply need to reach out and grab it.

References

1   Nature (2011) What is the Human Genome Worth? (11 May),
    www.nature.com/news/2011/110511/full/news.2011.281.html.
2   www.battelle.org/spotlight/5-11-11_genome.aspx.
3   Moorthy, V. S. et al. (2003) Safety and Immunogenicity of DNA/Modified
    Vaccinia Virus Ankara Malaria Vaccination in African Adults, *Journal of
    Infectious Diseases*, **188** (8) 1239–44.
4   Economic Analysis of Scientific Research Publishing (2003),
    www.wellcome.ac.uk/stellent/groups/corporatesite/@policy_communicati
    ons/documents/web_document/wtd003182.pdf; and Costs and Business
    Models in Scientific Research Publishing (2004),
    www.wellcome.ac.uk/stellent/groups/corporatesite/@policy_communicati
    ons/documents/web_document/wtd003184.pdf.
5   www.wellcome.ac.uk/About-us/Policy/Policy-and-position-
    statements/WTD002766.htm.
6   www.wellcome.ac.uk/About-us/Policy/Policy-and-position-
    statements/WTD002766.htm.
7   http://creativecommons.org/licenses/by/3.0/.
8   www.rcuk.ac.uk/documents/documents/2005statement.pdf.

9 www.rcuk.ac.uk/documents/documents/2006statement.pdf.

10 www.mrc.ac.uk/Ourresearch/Ethicsresearchguidance/
Openaccesspublishing/Positionstatement/index.htm.

11 www.bbsrc.ac.uk/web/FILES/Policies/access_research_outputs_update.pdf.

12 www.researchinfonet.org/publish/finch.

13 www.rcuk.ac.uk/media/news/2012news/Pages/120716.aspx.

14 www.openaire.eu/en/open-access/open-access-overview.

15 http://ec.europa.eu/research/science-society/document_library/pdf_06/
open-access-pilot_en.pdf.

16 http://grants.nih.gov/grants/guide/notice-files/NOT-OD-04-064.html.

17 http://poynder.blogspot.co.uk/2012/05/open-access-mandates-
ensuring.html.

18 www.taxpayeraccess.org/action/action_frpaa/FRPAA2012.shtml.

19 Davis, P. M. (2008) Open Access Publishing, Article Downloads, and
Citations: randomised controlled trial, *BMJ*, **337**, a568, http://ukpmc.ac.uk/
articles/PMC2492576.

20 http://chronicle.com/blogs/wiredcampus/jstor-tests-free-read-only-
access-to-some-articles/34908.

21 *Benefits to the Private Sector of Open Access to Higher Education and Scholarly
Research report*, http://open-access.org.uk/wp-content/
uploads/2011/10/OAIG_Benefits_OA_PrivateSector.pdf.

22 Lyman, S. (2011) Industry Access to the Literature, *Nature Biotechnology*, **29**,
571–92.

23 http://labs.ukpmc.ac.uk/evf.

24 RIN (2011) *Heading for the Open Road: costs and benefits of transitions in scholarly
communications*, www.rin.ac.uk/our-work/communicating-and-disseminating-
research/heading-open-road-costs-and-benefits-transitions-s.

25 http://project-soap.eu/report-from-the-soap-symposium.

26 http://blogs.plos.org/plos/2011/07/2010-plos-progress-update.

27 See www.infotoday.com/it/jan11/Interview-with-Derk-Haank.shtml, where
Derk Haank, CEO, Springer Science, states that 'BioMed Central has a very
healthy margin, more than double digits. It is not marginally profitable but a
very sound business.'

28 http://sca.jiscinvolve.org/wp/files/2009/07/sca_bms_casestudy_
hindawi.pdf.

29 www.subscription-agents.org/system/files/Robert%20Kiley%20ASA%
202011_0.ppt

30 http://en.wikipedia.org/wiki/Occupy_Wall_Street.

31 www.soros.org/openaccess.

32 For example, see http://ukpmc.blogspot.co.uk/2012/01/springerplus-new-oa-journal-from.html, and http://ukpmc.blogspot.co.uk/2011/10/open-biology-new-open-access-journal.html and http://cellreports.cell.com/.

33 A description of the goals of *eLife* can be found at http://wellcometrust.wordpress.com/2011/11/07/elife-a-journal-by-scientists-for-scientists/.

34 Department for Business, Innovation and Skills (2012) Letter to Dame Janet Finch on the Government response to the Finch Report: *Accessibility, Sustainability, Excellence: how to expand access to research publications*, www.gov.uk/government/uploads/system/uploads/attachment_data/file/32493/12-975-letter-government-response-to-finch-report-research-publications.pdf.

11

Changing institutional research strategies

Ian M. Carter

ABSTRACT

University research strategies make statements about research ambitions, but rarely speak directly about scholarly communications. At the same time, communication of all sorts has become central to a university, whether to support recruitment, present a public profile or respond to events. This chapter seeks to explore the relationship between institutional research strategies and scholarly communications and to see how each may have affected the other and how they might do so in the future. It describes the purpose and structure of an institutional research strategy, and how these are changing. It highlights the linkages between strategy, implementation plans and policies, where the latter encourage desired behaviours. In the context of scholarly communications, the research strategy is the public document in which an institution states its commitment to such forms of communication: that discovering new knowledge and sharing that discovery in meaningful ways are at the heart of the institution. The discussion then moves to the changing nature of scholarly communications, including the Open agenda, and questions how scholarly communications fits into the wider spectrum of institutional communications. The chapter concludes that there has probably been little direct connection between research strategies and approaches to scholarly communications, but that this is changing. Both institutions and individual researchers wish to demonstrate the quality, relevance and accessibility of their research, in order to be attractive to collaborators, funders and employers. Successful institutions will ensure that strategy and scholarly communications activities are mutually supportive, to the benefit of both their researchers and the organization.

Introduction

How have institutional research strategies affected scholarly communications, if at all?

How have changes in scholarly communications affected institutional research strategies?

This chapter addresses these two questions; and to that end it looks at the recent evolution of the institutional research strategy.

University research strategies (and their parent institutional strategies) have tended not to consider scholarly communication directly. Rather, they have tended to be statements about undertaking high-quality, relevant research and translating it into practice or other beneficial outcomes. It is implicit that the results of research will be disseminated, but little attention is paid to how, why and through what media.

At one level, this is neither surprising nor concerning. Indeed, the academic community might be more worried if their institutional strategy became too prescriptive. However, there are two related arguments to be made for a more explicit inclusion of scholarly communication in institutional research strategies.

The first is that we (and others) should not forget the centrality to their missions of high-quality scholarly enquiry and the development and dissemination of knowledge. Universities must retain these as core elements in their research strategies and thus explicitly state their commitment to them. Institutional commitments to open access to their research results fall under this heading, and are becoming more common. Recent government and funder policy statements reinforce this.[1]

The second is that the research strategy will need to address the interaction of the university's researchers and their research with broad, non-academic communities; hence, the appropriate forms of communication for these audiences will need to be explicit. There could be a danger that all institutional communication activity would concentrate on this area and, hence, not attempt to support the communication of the scholarly content to scholarly audiences. It is therefore important to articulate clearly the modes and purposes of communication in support of the research endeavour.

The institutional research strategy and policy infrastructure

Before discussing the connection of research strategy to scholarly communication, it is important to take account of the full panoply of institutional strategy and policy mechanisms and documentation, in order to understand the purposes and interrelationships of all the elements.

Strategies and operational plans provide the vision, end-points and specific actions. Policies should provide the desired behavioural environment: motivating staff to develop appropriate personal contributions. They need to be aligned with the strategic vision in terms of what is permitted, and with the implementation plan in terms of how it is delivered.

The 'need' for a research strategy

There has been an increasing need, or at least pressure, for institutions to have a research strategy, arising from a number of quarters:

- Research is increasingly carried out in a policy-driven environment, with governments and funders expecting or requiring an institution to have a strategy in order to qualify for funding.
- Institutions are becoming more active in managing their research, in particular as they have to address questions of resource prioritization.
- Greater levels of regulation and legislation need to be translated into the institutional policy framework.
- There is more interest in managing the whole lifecycle of research and knowledge exchange.

An example of externally driven strategy development was the introduction of the Joint Infrastructure Fund in 1998 by the UK Funding Bodies, the Research Councils and the Wellcome Trust. This scheme, which funded major research infrastructure such as buildings and large equipment, required an institution's research strategy to be submitted as part of any proposal so that alignment could be demonstrated across the sector. This led a number of universities to write their first explicit research strategies.

What is a research strategy?

A university's research strategy is often a formal, public document outlining the institution's goals and how it will measure its success in achieving them. By their nature, such documents can be bland, and end up trying to contain messages for different audiences, both internal and external. In some cases, they can amount to New Year's resolutions: aspirations that are not achievable, or that are not followed through.

There may, therefore, be one or more internal documents at institutional and departmental levels that are more detailed and that express more directly what is being planned. These are unlikely to be published outside the institution and may not even be fully revealed internally. At the institutional level strategies will be broad, whereas at a departmental level they are more likely to be a collection of individual and team aspirations, as that is the nature of the academic research environment.

A strategy may have targets for specific subject areas, although these are usually better stated at the departmental level than at the institutional level: 'being the best in X' can be difficult to substantiate; it can also be a hostage to fortune. Conversely, an institution can aim to provide the right environment for success, and might use a number of action areas or critical success factors, such as:

- people (recruiting, developing, rewarding and retaining)
- infrastructure (the physical environment and the human support structures)
- resources (having the funds to invest in the people and the infrastructure)
- institutional management (appropriate, motivational leaders at all levels, including succession planning)
- key strategic relationships (major interactions that determine ability to deliver or represent significant customers for a range of institutional products)
- market positioning (determining the type of organization one wants to be).

What makes it work?

A strategy needs to be meaningful to those whom it affects. This may mean a need for different versions for different audiences. This is not to say that the strategic direction will be different, just what is emphasized and how it is expressed. This is another reason for having both institutional and departmental strategies. Equally important is to have an implementation plan, as this identifies the specific tasks and actions that will be undertaken to make a difference. It is usually also easier to measure performance against the actions in the implementation plan than against the broader aspirations of the strategy.

The final necessary element is an enabling policy environment that motivates staff to develop their personal contributions (again reflecting the nature of academic research). Policies should define what is 'acceptable', what is 'expected' and how it will be rewarded. They might be divided into two categories: formal institutional policies that are part of an employee's terms and conditions of employment or a student's terms of registration; and operational mechanisms that define how processes should work.

Institutional policies include a wide range of areas, and are typically the way in which external regulation is implemented. Policies should provide a framework, with an amount of flexibility, for recognizing differences between subjects, the changing nature of the research environment and the interconnected nature of the drivers of individuals' behaviour.

Measuring progress

As already noted, measuring progress is easier against specific goals (did it happen? did it have the desired effect?), although the institutional strategy should have objectives with measurable targets. One can choose whether to measure inputs, outputs or outcomes, or a combination of these. Equally, one can measure absolute or comparative performance. Each has its place. Similarly, quality and volume of activity are both relevant (e.g., peer-review assessments, citations, postgraduate research student completions per academic, external income per academic); but so is having an understanding of the state of the infrastructure (hence, capital spend per academic can be tracked).

Connecting strategy and planning

One of the challenges that we face is the differing timescales of the processes. Strategy is often presented in terms of five or ten years, whereas most institutions have an annual planning process that may use a rolling three-year period but be linked to a one-year budgeting process (the latter in particular because of the cycle of allocations from government through the funding bodies).

Research is a highly complex, behavioural system that needs to be integrated, and managing creativity needs a subtlety of approach. All of the elements of the strategy and policy infrastructure need to point in the same direction, and to leave plenty of room for individual and organizational expression.

How might scholarly communication be represented in a research strategy?

The research strategy should be regarded as a public document in which an institution states its commitment to scholarly communication. It does not need to be detailed, but should lie at the heart of an institution's research and knowledge-exchange objectives. Having a clear statement reinforces the purpose of the research at the institution: to discover new knowledge and to share it in meaningful ways. Scholarly communications are about documenting and sharing discoveries. The current and future challenge is in ensuring that the sharing will be meaningful and plural.

Any statement on scholarly communication might be coupled with the institutional commitment to academic freedom, in terms of the freedom to express (informed) views. Scholarly outputs are one important form of embodiment of such expressions.

Perhaps a more interesting question relates to the purpose of scholarly communications, and how that might be changing. Some parts of the answer to this question will be the same as they were at the time of the first publication of *Philosophical Transactions* in 1665; other parts, however, might reflect different drivers. More specifically:

■ to publish the results of research, to assure their quality, and to enable their replication, understanding and use by others

- to provide information on specific projects and activities, and their outcomes
- to demonstrate areas of interest and capability, and hence to provide information for potential collaborators, funders or customers.

In the 17th, 18th and 19th centuries scholars tended to be polymaths, with significant applied interests. The trend through the 20th century was one of narrowing and deepening interests, yet combined with a desire to interact across disciplines. Separately, there have been societal (usually governmental) imperatives to enable the practical application of research. Institutional research strategies respond to each of these tendencies, seeking to demonstrate and support the depth, interconnectedness and transferability of research. In that context, what is the expectation of scholarly communications, and, indeed, of other forms of communication? Where does scholarly communication sit in a continuum of communications, and what relationship does it need to have to the other parts? It is certain that scholarly communication needs to be adequately integrated, rather than the research community believing that it can function in semi-isolation in order to preserve its purity.

Scholarly communication is not only about the dissemination of new knowledge to other scholars. It is (or certainly should be) about informed dissemination to a range of audiences, for multiple purposes. This is not to say that every item of communication has to be presented for a tabloid audience, but it should be understandable and accessible.

A recent report commissioned by the Joint Information Systems Committee on behalf of the Open Access Implementation Group[2] found that private sector users of scholarly outputs had difficulty in understanding the potential value of an article from the abstract, because of the way it was written. (The report was written in the context of access to scholarly output, on which more below. It found that discoverability and transparency were also issues, alongside ease of access.) This illustrates the inter-sectoral communication requirements, but similar comments might also apply to inter-disciplinary use of scholarly outputs within the academic sector. There is thus a responsibility on the sector and its members to ensure that scholarly outputs are understandable, including to non-traditional audiences. Ironically, perhaps, while there has been a growing market for coffee table books and TV programmes based on scholarly subjects and studies, these are possibly looked down upon by the purist. In the current UK context, they may not count for much in the assessment of outputs in the Research Excellence Framework (REF),[3] but, in terms of the (non-academic) impact element of that assessment, they might help to demonstrate public engagement.

One response to this this might be for institutions (or, perhaps better, publishers) to require a truly lay abstract of each article that is produced. Would that not demonstrate commitment to open scholarship, public engagement and inter-disciplinary transparency?

Repositories, Open Access and scholarly communication

Many institutions have established institutional repositories, partly to catalogue their research outputs and partly to provide access to the content, where permitted by the publishers' copyright. In doing so, an institution is likely to have introduced a policy on whether or not staff are required to record their research outputs in the repository – and some include an encouragement or requirement to deposit the full-text documents.

Such policy requirements may not be included in a research strategy, but, as discussed earlier, the policy should support a strategic objective, which will be recorded in the research strategy. The rise of the institutional repository is partly a consequence of the Open Access (OA) movement; but also because institutions are more concerned to ensure that they have a full knowledge of their scholarly outputs. This concern has been driven by external assessments such as the REF and its predecessors, and also by internal promotion and reward systems. These two are strategic drivers: to demonstrate quality and to retain high performers.

OA is promoted by a range of individuals and groups, but institutional responsibility, or evangelism even, often lies with the library, rather than being fully embedded in the research culture. The institutional research strategy (the public position statement) may have a role to play in this respect, but academic commitment to OA will only truly happen once the academic community believes that there is no negative effect (and, preferably, sees a positive effect) on their standing, and that there is no direct cost to them.

Where does scholarly communication fit in the wider institutional communications strategy?

Institutional communications have taken off in recent years, to promote the institution. However, the approach has varied from a student- and parent-centric one (to support recruitment), to public profile, to a reactive, damage-limitation process. In some cases, the institution promotes its research, but without targeting specific audiences. In others, the targets are clear.

University public relations (PR) offices typically seek to promote new scholarly publications, but the link between the researcher and the PR team is often weak. A journal article or book needs an amount of translation before it can be used in a general public context, and yet the timescale is often very tight because the PR team has not been alerted about the imminent publication. The latter is understandable, but certainly fixable in the majority of cases: there is often a considerable time lag between an article's being accepted for publication and being published. So, if an institution is capturing information during the development stages (rather than only after publication), then the institutional repository could automatically alert the PR team once an item is fit to be publicized. This would provide the PR team with a longer time in which to develop a better story and place it in a number of different media, and thus to enhance the reach of the scholarly article.

A related factor is the targeting of outlets. PR offices, naturally, tend to target the mainstream media, whether locally or nationally. While this has value, some also exercise more discrimination and seek to place items in relevant trade journals or in official documents. The call for vignettes to be embedded in official and semi-official publications is often at short notice; some PR offices seem to be better able to respond than others, and in doing so increase the visibility of their institution's research. This depends on having a good knowledge of the institution's research activities and outputs, and easy access to understandable summaries.

In developing an institutional research strategy and related infrastructure, one might consider developing ways to improve the communication of research, in order to provide some clarity (and performance measures) about the forms, frequency and volume of communications activity. Such a strategy might lead universities to consider not just the volume and quality of traditional forms of scholarly communications, but also how research is communicated to a variety of audiences, internal and external, using a variety of media.

Conclusions

To return to the opening questions: have institutional research strategies affected scholarly communications, and vice versa? There probably has not been that much effect in either direction, so far. This is beginning to change. The two trends will see greater linking between the institutional research strategy and scholarly communications. Universities are seeking to differentiate themselves, and their approaches to research communications and scholarly communications may help them to achieve this. An institution might ask itself how to make best use of its research in order to demonstrate quality, relevance and accessibility. What strategies, policies, processes and infrastructure should be in place?

Equally, individual researchers might ask themselves how they can ensure that their research appears in the best possible locations and formats, so that it is recognized by peers and potential collaborators, current and future employers, current and future funders, by those who might find it useful and by the general public both in this country and internationally.

This contrasting of institutional versus individual perspectives shows that it is in the institutional interest to ensure that the goals of individual researchers are met. The latter, after all, underpin the institutional research strategy and determine its success. Scholarly communications and institutional research strategies can and should indeed sit comfortably together. Successful institutions and individuals will ensure that the two are mutually supportive.

References

1   The Finch Working Group on Expanding Access to Published Research Findings published its report in July 2012, available at www.researchinfonet.org/wp-content/uploads/2012/06/Finch-Group-report-FINAL-VERSION.pdf, and made a number of recommendations that have been accepted by government. The government statement is available at www.bis.gov.uk/assets/biscore/science/docs/l/12-975-letter-

government-response-to-finch-report-research-publications.pdf, and the UK Research Councils' revised policy is at www.rcuk.ac.uk/research/ Pages/outputs.aspx. The European Commission has also announced its policy in this area, available at http://europa.eu/rapid/pressReleasesAction.do?reference=IP/12/790.

2   HOST Policy Research (2011) *Benefits to the Private Sector of Open Access to Higher Education and Scholarly Research: a Research Report to JISC (October)*, http://open-access.org.uk/wp-content/uploads/2011/10/OAIG_ Benefits_OA_PrivateSector.pdf.

3   REF is the UK's periodic national assessment of research quality, used to inform core research funding allocation. See www.hefce.ac.uk/research/ref.

12

The role of the research library

Mark L. Brown

ABSTRACT

Research libraries see themselves as being in the forefront of moves to extend, exploit and promote new forms of scholarly communication. The advent of the digital environment has created new opportunities for librarians to act as protagonists, advocates and innovators. The role of research librarians now extends beyond being facilitators, brokers and guardians, to working as champions of change for the benefit of the whole research community. Nationally and internationally, libraries are engaged in collaborative initiatives to find the best ways to support the research process and extend affordable access to the rapidly growing volume of resources that is now available. This chapter reviews the role of research libraries in responding to an increasingly complex research environment, and the response of libraries to the acceleration of digital publishing, escalating costs and the long-term preservation needs of research outputs, as well as their positioning in the debates on Open Access and research data management. Research libraries are bringing knowledge and professional expertise to the task of enhancing the effectiveness of the research environment, which is placing them in the role of advocates and service integrators. The success of this activity has been underpinned by a strengthening of the natural tendency of research libraries to form strong collaborative networks that can share knowledge, pursue joint initiatives and work co-operatively.

Introduction

Research libraries see themselves as being in the forefront of moves to extend, exploit and promote new forms of scholarly communication. This is not surprising, since their position as guardians of the scholarly record stretches back centuries, and libraries have often combined long-term perspectives with a commitment to innovation. The advent of the digital environment has created new opportunities for librarians to act as protagonists, advocates and innovators. The role of research librarians now extends beyond being facilitators, brokers and guardians, to working with other stakeholders as champions of change for the benefit of the whole research community.

The pace of change in the landscape of scholarly communication has created both significant opportunities and interesting challenges. The adoption of whole new areas of activity has transformed the way that research libraries position themselves. The 'library without walls' now includes digitization and discovery for research collections, advice and support for authors on citation and impact, fostering digital skills, shaping research data management strategies, managing research outputs and research metrics, digital preservation, institutional repositories, digital publishing and Open Access (OA). In the face of this wide agenda, the challenges for libraries are both local and international. Within their institutions, libraries are questioning long-held ideas about what constitutes the scholarly collection. In the areas of access and delivery they are continually reviewing the issues of service infrastructure, the relationship between the library and researchers and the level of knowledge and skill required of their workforce to deliver the full range of modern scholarly communication. Nationally and internationally, libraries are engaged in collaborative initiatives to optimize support for the research process and to extend affordable access to the rapidly growing volume of resources that is now available.

Expanding the library's role as guardian of collections

In terms of the scholarly communications lifecycle, research libraries have an established role as providers and curators of the scholarly record. As the concept of the research library collection has now permanently shifted from that of a physical entity to a more flexible concept combining print, virtual access and desktop delivery, libraries are responding by broadening their traditional role. Print and archive collections still remain core elements within any library's collections, but the ubiquity of the electronic journal, experiments with new forms of scholarly output and the increasing range of 'born digital' material, licensed rather than owned, together with the sheer volume of output, all pose issues for libraries. Libraries are shifting their emphasis from the notion of a local collection to one based on the primacy of access to as wide a range of material as possible. New services have been introduced, by integrating access to different content within one search interface, to help users to search for and locate material and that allows them to find and access material online whether it is owned by the library, licensed or freely available over the internet.[1] As document supply services such as those delivered by the British Library and consortia such as OCLC (Online Computer Library Center) have been streamlined to provide electronic delivery to the desktop, libraries have become more selective in what they purchase for their core collections.

Recognizing this shift in emphasis, libraries have moved beyond local solutions to a more collaborative model for access and preservation. The quest for access to scholarly material extends to services such as 'pay per view' and 'patron driven acquisition for monographs', and libraries are experimenting with national or consortia agreements to optimize access and share costs.[2] UK academic libraries are also fortunate in having a national body, JISC (Joint Information Systems Committee) Collections, spearheading national negotiations to optimize licences and achieve standard pricing structures and contract terms (www.jisc-collections.ac.uk). JISC Collections has been invaluable to the sector not only in negotiating framework agreements, but also in purchasing high-value resources that are beyond the financial reach of individual libraries and in commissioning infrastructure enhancements which support better management and promotion of electronic collections.

This changing emphasis is also raising significant questions about the long-term curation and preservation of the scholarly record. As much digital material is licensed rather than owned, libraries have been engaged in initiatives to ensure that there are robust solutions to the challenge of long-term preservation. Libraries are supporting the work being undertaken by national libraries such as the British Library[3] and the Royal Library of the Netherlands, international initiatives such as CLOCKSS (www.clockss.org/clockss/home) and PORTICO (www.portico.org/

digital-preservation/), and locally applied technologies such as LOCKSS (www.lockssalliance.ac.uk). In terms of institutional decision making, the support of national agencies such as the Digital Curation Centre in the UK is important in helping institutions to work collaboratively to identify issues and actions for long-term sustainability (www.dcc.ac.uk). Libraries are conscious that decisions made locally have a significant effect on long-term access. A good example of this in the UK is the UK Research Reserve (www.ukrr.ac.uk) project, through which individual libraries can make decisions on retention with some certainty about the long-term availability of text in the context of a national programme co-ordinated through the British Library.

Whereas research libraries continue to take a long-term view of the significance of the scholarly record, one of the consequences of this broadening of activity is that they have been led to engage more closely with the issues associated with licensing, long-term costs and business models, as well as author and institutional rights. As their role diversifies, they are also adopting new perspectives as content creators, proxy authors and publishers which go beyond the relationship between a research library and a university press. These differing roles can be challenging. In the context of licensing models for their own digital outputs, libraries have to consider models for sustainability as well as access, and as digital publishers they have to grapple with the full range of challenges. In turn, this trend is fostering new knowledge and skills, which is improving the quality of the advice available from librarians to researchers on the issues of intellectual property rights (IPR), copyright and licensing.

This engagement also extends to the contribution that libraries are making in the area of research training. In response to UK funder requirements, particularly in the area of doctoral training and institutional commitment to supporting research careers, research training in the UK is an expanding area of activity. Libraries now offer courses and one-to-one support on topics such as bibliometrics and research analytics, responding to funder mandates and publishing, IPR and copyright, in order to support researchers in interpreting the publishing landscape. The integration of this offer within the overall training environment for researchers is important for the future, as the complexities of publication, citation analytics and impact have to be interpreted in an institutional context. Libraries are increasingly working more closely with research support offices within their institutions to respond to these demands.

This changing concept of the library and its collections is therefore placing the library more firmly within the research environment. Libraries are now engaged with the broader issues of scholarly communication, including publication media, visibility and impact, and the extent to which the current publication model is able to satisfy these needs. This leads them to ask fundamental questions about the nature of scholarly publishing and the long-term financial models which sustain it.

Responding to the publishing deluge

Access to journal articles, conference proceedings and other forms of scholarly communication is crucial for research. Faced with an increasing range of potential material, researchers regard their access to scholarly content as too limited.[4] Pressed by government and funder initiatives to drive up quality and impact, researchers have now to function both as consumers and as producers of scholarly content. This has presented research libraries with a dilemma: as the pressure on academics to publish and the continual upward swing of technological innovation have spawned more and more content, libraries face ever-increasing costs because funding for peer-reviewed journals, the primary vehicle for scholarly communication, takes a larger and larger share of their budgets. The disjunction between increases in journal costs and increases in library budgets internationally has been well documented.[5]

One of the most visible expressions of the role of research libraries as protagonists in the development of new forms of scholarly communication is in the collective response to what has been termed the 'serials crisis', in which major research libraries in the UK and the USA struggle to reconcile the ever-increasing demands of researchers for access to content with the sustained high inflation of journal subscriptions. For librarians, this dilemma lies at the heart of their role as providers of the widest possible access to the widest possible range of material to the widest possible community. Whereas access to print worked within certain well-understood limitations, users now expect fast, comprehensive access to everything, delivered on demand to the desktop. Many users perceive that, in one way or another, everything is, and should be, freely and openly accessible. This is in stark contrast to the realities of electronic scholarly publishing. For libraries do not own a growing part of the material in their collections; rather, they subscribe to it on behalf of a defined community, who are bound by licence provisions that are complex, that can be unpredictable in terms of cost and that are often not aligned with the diversifying business models within higher education.

Research libraries have therefore taken the view that it is important to challenge those business models which do not provide the flexibility that their users increasingly expect and which do not accord with financial realities. In this response they have gained the support of researchers who are concerned that the traditional models may limit opportunities to make their scholarship visible to the widest possible audience, and who are seeking to speed up the whole process of publication. Here again, expectations are running ahead of models developed in the context of print and which, despite the migration to electronic delivery, are perceived by researchers and librarians not to have fully adjusted to the potential of the electronic environment.

The lure of OA

It is no accident, therefore, that research libraries have investigated alternative options, and have become identified with projects to diversify the market and to promote OA to scholarly communication. There is a strong collaborative element to this trend, both among libraries and between libraries and researchers. In the UK this has been spearheaded by JISC, which has acted as a focus for experimenting with sustainable change. The JISC OA vision acknowledges that 'cultural change, policy development, technical infrastructure and sustainable business models are all needed in a transition to open access' (www.jisc.ac.uk/openaccess). It is the opportunity to provide institutions with a framework for change in these four key areas that research libraries have been keen to embrace.

One area where libraries have been very active is with regard to research repositories, the Green OA model. In many institutions the university library has taken the initiative in developing and promoting the research repository as a way to increase the visibility of its university's research, meet funders' mandates and provide researchers with an opportunity to expose their research early in the publication cycle. At institutional level, the value of the research repository has been strongly identified with a university's strategies for the Research Assessment Exercise/Research Excellence Framework, identifying the repository as an integral part of the research management systems.[6] For libraries, the opening up of content through harvesting services such as Google Scholar is part of the wider strategy for access and resource sharing. Libraries have also promoted national initiatives to extend the reach of repositories to less accessible material such as working papers, conference proceedings and, in particular, theses (www.ethos.ac.uk).

In identifying themselves with this approach research libraries have found themselves in contention with publishers, but on the whole this contention has been creative in advancing the debates on scholarly communication. Libraries are keen to derive benefits for their users from the policy initiatives emerging from funders such as Research Councils UK and the Wellcome Trust, and from government agencies in the US and the EU, to make publicly funded research more widely available internationally. This, in turn, has led to initiatives to test the boundaries around current publication models and to exploit the willingness of researchers to engage in new forms of scholarly communication.[7] As well as taking the lead in advocacy and promotion and in working closely with their research communities, libraries have engaged nationally and internationally in initiatives to extend the range of repository content and to support options for the early release of scholarly research. In terms of success, the widely held inherent trust in the library as providing a long-term commitment to the scholarly record has been a significant element in gaining traction for these models within institutions.

But although research libraries have been very active in the promotion of the Green OA model,[8] it has to be acknowledged that, except in specific disciplines with an established tradition of subject archiving, the combination of publishers' restrictions and the limits of researchers' commitment to self-archiving has meant that the Green model is often seen as extending rather than replacing the traditional scholarly publication with full peer review. However, the appearance of more demanding funder mandates for OA to publicly funded research has promoted debate on issues such as the acceptable length of embargo periods before material can be made Green OA. At the same time, it has prompted more interest in the Gold OA model.

Research libraries have been keen to link content in the increasing number of OA journals into their discovery services,[9] but have tended to take a more sceptical stance towards the author-pays business model for hybrid journals.[10] On the one hand Gold OA has strong appeal in making more content available in traditional journals with the long-established and valued formats for peer review, impact and citation analytics. Despite the analysis set out in the Houghton Report,[10] that a move to Gold OA could, in principle, reduce net costs to the UK research sector, the transition model for current subscription-based journals remains undefined, and the level of authors' submission charges discourages researchers from adopting the author-pays model even in areas where submission charges may be recoverable from the funder. It is hard to see how the increased costs of paying authors' charges will be outweighed by a proportionate fall in subscription payments, in the short term at least.[11] This is particularly the case for the major research libraries that currently subscribe to the Big Deals from the major publishers.

Nonetheless, some research libraries have been experimenting more directly with shaping policies and promoting institutional funding streams for the author-pays model as a focus for responding to funder mandates to make research outputs publicly available.[12] Even if the institution opts not to establish a central fund, the library is often seen as a valuable interpreter of the OA landscape, its advice being sought by research committees charged with establishing institutional policy. This role will extend as the landscape becomes more complex, particularly in the UK as a result of the recommendations of the 2012 Finch Report.[13] The Finch Report sets out a challenge to funders, institutions and researchers to embrace Gold OA for the UK as a means to make UK research more visible, to encourage other countries to follow the UK's lead and to increase market pressure on publishers to rebalance their subscription economies. The report envisages that several different channels for communicating research results will remain important over the next few years and acknowledges the value of repositories for 'grey literature', but recommends a clear policy direction in the UK towards support for OA publishing. We may expect research libraries to play a significant role in the debate on the Finch Report's recommendations.

Grappling with research data

Although much of the debate on OA has centred on published outputs, the same issues are now being explored in the area of research data.[14] It may not be immediately obvious why research libraries are adopting a high-profile approach to research data as part of their role in scholarly communication.[15] The fact is that research libraries do not see themselves as a new breed of institutional data managers; rather, their aim is to contribute to the development of a cross-institutional model for managing their researchers' data, fostering stronger links between researchers and supporting services and thus shaping an integrated approach to service delivery. For this reason they are playing a crucial role in projects and pilot studies to make the research-data landscape easier to navigate and to meet funders' requirements for OA to publicly funded research.

Research libraries can contribute their knowledge and professional experience in managing elements of the research environment, including repository management, metadata, training and advocacy, promotion and publication and digital preservation.[16] In the area of data management, libraries are promoting the concept of a cross-service team in which the computing service contributes complementary expertise in data storage, transmission, migration, security and authentication, and the research office has responsibility for research integrity, IPR, costing and links with funders and commercial partners. Libraries have been active in the formulation and promotion of institutional data management policies and guidance, and are seen as taking a broad view of the data landscape. This is a very fast-moving area of interest for research libraries and the skills required in order to offer an effective service are very much at the forefront of debate.

Conclusion

Research libraries are playing an active role in innovation in scholarly communications. However, it is legitimate to ask to what extent this activity is enhancing services for researchers and building new opportunities for the future. Not all innovation necessarily leads to success, but there are three main ways in which active engagement by research libraries is expanding horizons.

First, research libraries are acting as a spearhead for experimentation and advocacy within their institutions. They are acknowledged to have a role in managing and expanding the range of material in institutional repositories; they are seen as centres of knowledge and expertise for interpreting the issues of Green and Gold OA; and they are now extending this strategic role to the area of research data management. These are all examples of research libraries successfully working in creative ways to make it easier to build the infrastructure that is needed in order to increase the internal and external visibility of scholarly communications. Repositories are now part of the scholarly communication landscape, and this is in no small part due to the commitment of research libraries to lead institutionally in this area. We may expect the same level of engagement with regard to research data management.

Second, research libraries have been working assiduously to maximize access to all forms of scholarly communication. Whereas content may be seen as being freely available on the web, libraries remain key brokers in an increasingly complex digital environment where access is a function of licensing and the sophistication of the delivery infrastructure. Libraries have been leading initiatives to expand the range of content and to contain costs. Initiatives have included engaging in national frameworks for content acquisition, bringing material forward for digitization, experimenting with new business models for scholarly monographs and creating open content for material such as theses, working papers and other grey literature. This has fostered the acquisition of knowledge and expertise in the areas of access and licensing, and places research libraries in an influential position within institutions in identifying and negotiating best value.

Third, much of the success of this activity has been underpinned by a strengthening of the natural tendency of research libraries to form strong collaborative networks in order to pool resources, share knowledge, pursue joint initiatives and work in co-operation. In the UK the Research Information Network investigates the landscape, the JISC develops national-level initiatives and services and the membership organizations Research Libraries UK and SCONUL (the Society of College, National and University Libraries) develop the culture of collective action across the sector. This brings a value above that which is provided by an individual research library and provides a focus for development that is able to achieve more through the strategic use of networks.

As a result of their engagement with the increasing diversity within scholarly communication, research libraries are playing an ever more integral role in the research lifecycle, broadening their role as advocates, brokers and innovators.

References

1 Research Information Network (2006) *Researchers and Discovery Services: behaviour, perceptions, needs*, www.rin.ac.uk/our-work/using-and-accessing-information-resources/researchers-and-discovery-services-behaviour-perc.

2 An example of this is the Scottish Higher Education Digital Library (SHEDL), which was the subject of a recent evaluation impact study. Research Information Network (2010) *Evaluating the Impact of SHEDL*, www.rin.ac.uk/our-work/using-and-accessing-information-resources/evaluating-impact-shedl.

3 www.bl.uk/aboutus/stratpolprog/ccare/introduction/digital.

4 Research Information Network (2011) *Access to Scholarly Content: gaps and barriers*, www.rin.ac.uk/node/1172.

5 www.rluk.ac.uk/content/background-briefing-proposed-action-reduce-journal-prices-member-libraries.

6 In 2011 JISC published case studies from Southampton and Salford on institutional response to open access, www.jisc.ac.uk/whatwedo/topics/opentechnologies/openaccess/institutionsandoa.aspx.

7 For a summary of the issues arising for the EU's Horizon 2010 and Open Access, see http://news.sciencemag.org/scienceinsider/2012/05/horizon-2020-a-80-billion-battle.html.

8 The Registry of Open Access Repositories (ROAR) lists 148 repositories in UK research institutions or departments, http://roar.eprints.org/cgi/roar_search/advanced?location_country=gb&software=&type=institutional&order=-recordcount%2F-date.

9 The Directory of Open Access Journals (DOAJ) provides a listing, www.doaj.org.

10 The complexities of transition were set out in the Houghton Report, Houghton, J. W. et al. (2009) *Economic Implications of Alternative Scholarly Publishing Models: exploring the costs and benefits*. JISC, www.jisc.ac.uk/publications/reports/2009/economicpublishingmodelsfinalreport.aspx. The subsequent 2011 report by the RIN emphasized the need to promote both models: Cook, J. et al. (2011) *Heading for the Open Road: costs and benefits*

of transitions in scholarly communications, RIN, www.rin.ac.uk/our-work/communicating-and-disseminating-research/heading-open-road-costs-and-benefits-transitions-s.

11 Cross estimated the current global average cost per article as £2634.

12 For a very comprehensive summary of the issues see Pinfield, S. (2010) Paying for Open Access? Institutional funding streams and OA publication charges, *Learned Publishing*, **23**, 39–52, http://m.friendfeed-media.com/1acb4475607910fe97653cf4d94936f5e48adb92.

13 www.researchinfonet.org/publish/finch.

14 Examples of funder policies include the National Institutes of Health in the United States, http://grants.nih.gov/grants/sharing.htm, RCUK in the UK, www.rcuk.ac.uk/research/Pages/DataPolicy.aspx, and in Germany on-going work by the FDG, Deutsche Forschungsgemeinschaft. The European Union is also promoting the use of public data from public bodies in the EU, http://ec.europa.eu/information_society/policy/psi/docs/pdfs/directive_proposal/2012/open_data.pdf.

15 Research Libraries UK (RLUK) was one of the primary project sponsors for the HEFCE-funded UKRDS project, www.ukrds.ac.uk, and research libraries have been significant partners in the current range of institutional projects funded by JISC in the linked Managing Research Data Programme which runs from 2009 to 2013: www.jisc.ac.uk/whatwedo/programmes/mrd.aspx and www.jisc.ac.uk/whatwedo/programmes/di_researchmanagement/managingresearchdata.aspx.

16 In 2012 RLUK held an event to explore some of these issues. Available at: www.rluk.ac.uk/content/clarifying-roles-libraries-research-data-management-discussion-day-find-creative-solutions.

13

The library users' view

Roger C. Schonfeld

ABSTRACT

This chapter focuses on scholars, rather than on all library users. In it I examine some of the key changes in scholarly practices and associated attitudes in recent years. What are some of the key aspects of the relationship between the academic library and those scholars who may make use of its collections and services? Against a shifting background of significant increases in the accessibility of a variety of information sources and services, how is that relationship changing? I will attempt to examine what it might mean to think of scholars as having the identity of 'library users', ultimately arguing that there has been a structural readjustment in the nature of the user's relationship with information services providers, including the library. The perspective presented in this chapter is rooted to some degree in the US higher education community. There, it has become clear in recent years that the principal differentiator among faculty members' attitudes and practices is discipline, far more than institutional type, years in the field or other characteristics. In 2012, Ithaka S+R is conducting research programmes with components in both the USA and the UK. So far, these have identified no evidence of any essential differences in the views of academics in the UK and the USA that would bear substantively on the issues covered in this chapter.

Introduction

As previous chapters have made clear, scholars today have a vastly increased number of options available to them to meet their information services needs. The academic library has responded with a variety of new infrastructures, services and strategies. An understanding of the users' views is ultimately vital for any information services organization that wishes to serve them.

Background

The nature of the scholar's relationship with information services organizations is, and always has been, multi-faceted. This relationship incorporates functions such as discovery of information, access to collections and the range of services necessary both to enable their use and to enable original research.

Traditionally, these functions were best, if not exclusively, provided in person. Discovery involved such tools as the card catalogue and reference collections. Collections of books, journals and other materials were usually developed for the ideal of locally maintained, on-site stacks.[1] Services included the staffed reference desk, bibliographers with research expertise dedicated to individual fields and other advanced reference services.

The geography of these functions had several impacts. In every case, local visits by the scholar to the library were required, yielding regular interactions with staff, both formal and informal. This allowed librarians to understand the practices and needs of a significant proportion of users. The library actually served as a visible intermediary, and at times a gateway, in providing access to a variety of collections and services. The local proximity of the library's services and its collections gave it a monopoly, or something close to that, in serving as scholars' principal 'interlocutor' for information services. It was possible to understand scholars as, in the first place, 'library users'.

Many traditional services and collections are now offered online, and so the overall relationship of users to their campus library and a variety of other information services providers has for some time been in transition. In the following sections I shall examine two groups of faculty member users – humanities researchers and scientists – to explore overall changes in their scholarly communications attitudes, behaviours and needs, with a focus on the higher education context in the USA. Comparing these disciplinary groupings is a useful way of showing some aggregate differences, but for service-planning purposes there are also important distinctions at the level of individual disciplines and sub-fields. At the level of disciplinary groupings, however, it is possible to analyse faculty members' changing relationship with a variety of information services providers, including their campus library.

Scientists

Over the past two decades, scientists (and many social scientists) have seen the very nature of their work change tremendously. Vast increases in the availability of computing resources and the collection of and provision of access to new data sources have significantly changed research methodologies in a number of fields. In their scholarly communication, scientists have adopted many new methods, both as authors and as readers, that are reshaping the landscape.

In both maintaining current awareness and conducting targeted research in the literature of one's field, new methods have increased the speed and efficiency of these discovery processes. Advanced alerting features can focus on topics of interest rather than issue-level tables of contents, thereby supplanting current-issues browsing as a principal way of maintaining current awareness. Targeted literature reviews are most likely to be conducted via online services like PubMed, Scopus, Web of Science, Google Scholar and even Google itself. The library pays for access to some of these discovery services, but it has typically been unable to learn very much about how its users exploit them or what needs this might indicate. The discovery services themselves, which in some cases also serve as content platforms, have significant information about user behaviours and interests, especially when there is a 'signed in' state that associates activity across sessions. Relative to the journal title to which a researcher may have subscribed, or the current issues of which a scientist may have regularly consulted, the content platform itself may in some cases be developing a relationship.

With respect to collections, the print-to-electronic transition has swept through scholarly journals in the sciences. Many research libraries have ceased collecting science journals in print whenever suitable electronic versions are available,[2] and increasingly they have been electing to eliminate their print backfile collections, especially when suitable digitized versions are made available.[3] New models of scientific book publishing have already seen some libraries indicate that they prefer electronic versions only, whenever possible.

With collections providing a declining rationale for library visits in person, and in an era of university austerity and campus space constraints, some libraries have reduced the physical space allotted to science branches or eliminated collections storage as a function.[4] Indeed, it is not uncommon for libraries to eliminate the physical presence of one or more science branches.[5] In many cases, the reductions in physical presence are linked with a stated commitment to re-energize the services provided; the impact of such developments on the library relationship with scientists is not yet well understood.

Yet the library invests significantly in the sciences. Many academic libraries expend a disproportionate share of their materials budgets (on a per-academic basis) on the sciences. In the past several decades the share of library materials budget devoted to the sciences has typically grown significantly, largely owing to the relatively higher price increases for materials in STEM disciplines.[6]

Libraries have responded to price increases with a variety of advocacy campaigns and negotiating strategies, ultimately raising awareness among scientists of the pricing and access issues that have long frustrated librarians. As a result of these awareness-building campaigns, scientists are more likely than they once were to know that the library spends significant resources to give them access to their fields' formal scholarly communications.

Even so, due to changing discovery and delivery practices, these materials (a significant proportion of library spending) are today almost exclusively used in research processes that are removed from an environment in which scientists will be aware of the added value that has been provided by the library. The library typically expends a great deal of effort in acquiring these materials, as well as in providing discovery services and vital infrastructure to knit them together seamlessly for users. But the scientist, for whom the experience is indeed frequently seamless, has little recognition that he is using the campus library, other than in its role as a purchasing agent.

That user may, however, vividly experience other service providers. For example, a discovery service or content platform may regularly send highly targeted alerts to registered users, and in many cases one of these services will have become a regular starting-point in a given scholar's research process. Other tools, such as reference-management services like Zotero, document-management and collaboration-support services like Mendeley, and even principally non-academic services like the cloud storage service Dropbox, may seem to have introduced an element of magic into the scholar's research routine.

A snapshot of these changes in the scientist's perception of the valued roles of the academic library in recent years, from the Ithaka S+R Faculty Survey, is provided in Figure 13.1. The increase in scientists' awareness of the library as a purchaser, and its concurrent declining role as a gateway, are both striking.[7]

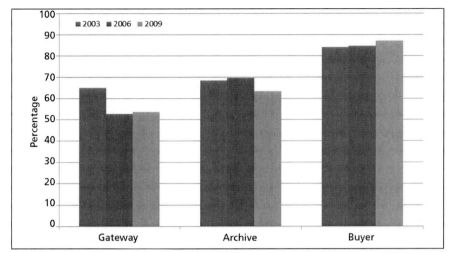

Figure 13.1 Importance of selected academic library functions among scientists

To sum up, user affinity has shifted significantly in recent years. Whereas once the library was the principal information services organization in the scientist's research process, today the picture is more complex. It would not be surprising if many scientists were to express a growing affinity for a variety of services that provide content, personalized discovery and research tools, but that exist outside the library.[8]

Humanities researchers

For humanities researchers several key elements are sufficiently different from those facing scientists that they reflect a rather different dynamic, at least for the time being. There is a significant community of humanities researchers utilizing research methods enabled by computational analysis of large-scale data sets, but there are also many who have elected to continue to use the traditional methods that have served them well over time and in which the library plays a significant role. Due to the monograph-oriented nature of many humanities fields, mechanisms for current awareness and targeted literature reviews have not changed as radically as they have for scientists. A key question is the extent to which upcoming developments may foster change for these scholars too.

In many fields, humanities researchers have traditionally relied on monographs at least as much as on journals for scholarly communication.

The long-form narrative format of the monograph has been especially well suited for broad, summative analyses in fields like history and literature. There may be certain pressures threatening to overturn this precedent, such as a growing desire to communicate ideas more quickly, and the challenges imposed by the economics of monograph publishing. Still, overall, humanities fields remain far more monograph-reliant than do the sciences.

Discovery practices have historically been informed to a significant degree by format. For targeted literature reviews, these researchers are comparatively reliant upon the library catalogue and other resources containing information about monographs. Current awareness may frequently be maintained through the book reviews that are an important element of many humanities journals.

But even given their continued reliance on monographs, discovery practices have begun to shift for humanities researchers, as illustrated by findings from the Ithaka S+R Faculty Survey in Figure 13.2. Humanities researchers increasingly turn to Amazon and Google Books for discovery purposes, rather than to a library catalogue. There has been a significant growth in review media outside scholarly journals' book reviews, through services like H-Net. While humanities researchers have not ceased to view the library catalogue as an important starting-point for their research, they are gradually moving towards externally provided services.

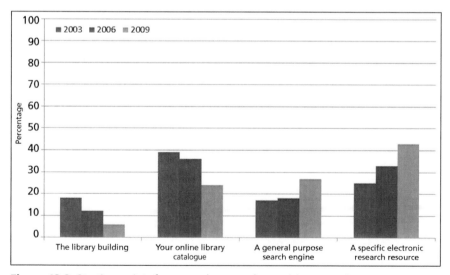

Figure 13.2 Starting-points for research among humanities researchers

At the same time, monograph publishers such as university presses are currently considering the prospect of publishing online editions. There are challenges yet to be resolved for some monographs, such as permissions for certain types of images and the pricing of prescribed texts. There are also opportunities, such as dramatically improved discovery and the opportunity to rethink the relationship between discrete chapters and the work as a whole. If online access to scholarly monographs proves not merely to supplement but actually to supplant the need for access to print versions, we may expect to see significant additional disruption. For example, while discussions to date about a print-to-electronic transition for library collections of scholarly monographs have been largely tentative,[9] there is growing interest among university library directors in exploring strategies for redesigning the provision of such collections. At this point, the data does not exist to speculate on how the needs of humanities researchers will change.

In their relationships with humanities researchers, libraries have another significant asset that has typically been absent in the case of scientists: a clear precedent in supporting not only secondary research but also original work. For example, archives are a vital source for many humanities researchers. Some research libraries gather oral histories, ephemera and other special collections, either to support centres of excellence in targeted areas or more broadly. Collections of rare books are essential to some fields, while for much literary scholarship the novels, poems and other published collections that form an essential part of the library's general collections are a primary source. When reference is made to the library serving as the 'laboratory of the humanities', these collections – both at the local campus library and also those that can be accessed at libraries worldwide – spring immediately to mind.

For these essentially primary source collections, the progress of digitization has accelerated substantially. Numerous initiatives have been mounted over the past decade and beyond to digitize library special collections and rare books, both by individual libraries and through projects like ProQuest's Early English Books Online and Gale's Eighteenth Century Collections Online. Mass digitization initiatives through Google, Microsoft and the Internet Archive have digitized not only substantial quantities of secondary source materials but, for the humanities, vital primary sources as well. In addition to more pervasive access to these materials (as a result of their availability to additional institutions and through enhanced bibliographic access), opportunities are being steadily developed for computational access through, for example, the HathiTrust Research Center, unlocking a variety of digital humanities applications.

It is as a result of the digitization and online availability of monograph and primary source collections that libraries and scholars in the humanities may see the most significant shifts in the nature of their relationship with one another. Many libraries express an increasing willingness, coupled with associated infrastructural and policy preferences, to treat digitized collections as a broader community resource, ubiquitously available without regard for institutional provenance, as far as possible. This choice, driven by a desire to increase access while collaborating deeply in order to minimize costs and provide quality services, may enable humanities researchers to adopt the same types of platforms, discovery services and research tools as have their scientific peers.

In the humanities, new types of research support services are being developed, especially in support of new types of research methods and practices. For example, many universities have created digital humanities centres, both inside the library organization and elsewhere on campus. These services may, over time, play a significant role in serving the research support needs of such researchers pursuing new types of research methods.[10]

Conclusion

In this chapter, I have taken two cases – the humanities and the sciences – to allow me to generalize the diversity of paths forward across numerous scholarly fields at a diversity of institutions. At the same time, I have ignored a variety of other user groups, such as students, in order to allow for this focus. Key trends regarding the user relationship emerge.

Some have interpreted the changing user relationship for information services that is indicated here as ultimately a marketing challenge for libraries, while others believe that it indicates more deeply structural change. While there are a variety of ways in which libraries have begun to address the marketing challenge, I have suggested in this chapter that there is a structural readjustment in the nature of the user relationship with information services providers, not only for scientists but perhaps also for humanities researchers as well.

This readjustment affords new opportunities for a variety of information services organizations and provides additional service points both for science and, increasingly, for the humanities. The productivity of scholars is increasing, and opportunities are growing for them to pursue new kinds of research questions.

For the library, which has far less of a monopoly on serving the needs of the scholar than it once did, a key question is how to ensure that the values that it has long stewarded on behalf of its user communities are maintained in this new environment. What services must the library offer, or at least be positioned to influence, in order to protect these values? For scholarly users, will the library principally focus on developing and preserving collections – locally generated as well as remotely acquired – while yielding various components of the services bundle to other providers? Or will it continue to pursue additional roles in order to support discovery, professional identity and presence, and a variety of other services, not only for humanities scholars but for the sciences as well? Depending on the vision that is being pursued for the academic library, it may be more or less important to ensure that the library's relationship with scholars is established on a sure footing.

References

1   Although inter-library loan developed as an early cross-institutional service that quickly encouraged many libraries to pursue as much creativity as the information-sharing infrastructure of the time could bear in rethinking locally maintained collections. Given the limitations of that infrastructure, most collections were developed and remained available principally, if not exclusively, for local use.

2   Libraries define 'suitable' based on local needs. For example, considerations at some libraries can include issues as diverse as digital preservation and post-cancellation rights, image and digitization quality, and content-provider type and terms of access.

3   Some key initiatives for collective planning around sharing print retention responsibilities and expanding availability while reducing aggregate costs include Project WEST (www.cdlib.org/services/west/) and the UK Research Reserve (www.ukrr.ac.uk/). Housewright, R. and Schonfeld, R. (2009) *What to Withdraw: print collections management in the wake of digitization* maps out a framework for system-wide analysis and decision making in these transitions (see www.sr.ithaka.org/research-publications/what-

withdraw-print-collections-management-wake-digitization/).

4 Competing claims to be the first bookless library, emphasizing the leadership of the University of Texas-San Antonio's engineering library, are indicative of the desire among some institutions to move in this direction. See Kolowich, S. (2010) A Truly Bookless Library, *Inside Higher Ed*, (17 September), www.insidehighered.com/news/2010/09/17/libraries.

5 Some examples in recent years include the Cornell physical sciences library and the Johns Hopkins medical library. See Kelley, M. (2011) Major Medical Library Closing Its Doors to Patrons and Moving to Digital Model, *The Digital Shift*, (27 October), www.thedigitalshift.com/2011/10/research/major-medical-library-closing-its-doors-to-patrons-and-moving-to-digital-model/; and Lin, E. (2009) Physical Sciences Library Prepares for Closure, *Cornell Daily Sun*, (4 December), http://cornellsun.com/section/news/content/2009/12/04/physical-sciences-library-prepares-closure.

6 Especially at non-research academic libraries, these price increases have often been accompanied by a significant increase in access to additional journal titles. Schonfeld, R. C., King, D. W., Okerson, A. and Fenton, E. G. (2004) *The Non-subscription Side of Periodicals: changes in library operations and costs between print and electronic formats.* Council on Library and Information Resources, figure 1, p. 13. Available at www.clir.org/pubs/abstract/pub127abst.html.

7 Schonfeld, R. C. and Housewright, R. (2010) *Faculty Survey 2009: strategic insights for librarians, publishers, and societies*, Ithaka S+R, http://bit.ly/cFtcsB.

8 Ithaka S+R's project on research support services for UK chemists examined these questions in 2012 with support from JISC (the Joint Information Systems Committee).

9 See Kieft, R. and Payne, L. (2010) A Nation-wide Planning Framework for Large-scale Collaboration on Legacy Print Monograph Collections, *Collaborative Librarianship*, **2** (4), http://collaborativelibrarianship.org/index.php/jocl/article/view/119.

10 Ithaka S+R's project on research support services for US historians examined these questions in 2012 with support from the National Endowment for the Humanities.

Index